Property Sale
In a Foreign Country

Property Sale in a Foreign Country

Global Property Sale–Florida as an Example

Andrea Hoff-Domin

DEDICATION

This book is dedicated to my uncle (my biological father's brother) and his family. They bestowed me their love and assistance when I needed that the most.

Information about the Author:

Born on October 6th in Lower Saxony, Germany. She tragically lost her father as a baby and her grandparents, especially her grandfather, had a big influence on her attitude towards life and her vision of the world. Books about foreign countries and their culture fascinated her since her childhood and prompted the wish to gather own experiences in this area. In order to make these experiences, she took a profession in the financial sector and subsequently worked in the IT-banking and real estate field. She gathered experience in foreign cultures and business processes in more than 30 countries around the world and more than 20 states in the United States.

Today she is the CEO of an international brokerage in Florida, remodels properties and focuses on cultural diversity and differences in life and business in the United States, Caribbean and Europe. For several years she publishes her experiences in books and on the internet. Her life motto is "Do, or do not. There is no try" (Star Wars – Yoda).

www.florida-dream-homes.net
www.andreahoffdomin.com
andrea@florida-informations.com

Inhalt

YOU OWN PROPERTY IN FLORIDA AND WANT TO SELL IT—WHAT IS THE BEST WAY TO DO IT?

A few years ago, as the market values of properties were at their deepest point, we showed you with our book Your Residence in Paradise the enormous potential of a property purchase in Florida. In that book, the focus was to explain a purchase transaction in the beautiful Sunshine State of Florida.

To find the property—a house or condominium (condo)—of your dreams and longings was our goal. Maybe at that time, a single-family home with a pool, dock, and direct connection to the open waters was your dream. Or maybe it was a condo with an unobstructed view of the endless horizon of the ocean and its breathtaking sunrises. Or maybe you dreamed of a property at the Intracoastal Waterway with a dock, a view of the city lights flickering under the sun setting in the west, and you with a glass of champagne in your hand.

Whatever your personal dream was at that time, our lives are always moving on, and our expectations and dreams are changing constantly. Things that we love today are no longer important tomorrow, or we find better goals that are more promising and attractive to us.

Another goal may be that you want to realize your gain from the property purchase in the past. That is understandable and comprehensible. You do not need to be ashamed of this feeling; it is just a business decision. It is just as if you were to buy a stock cheaply and resell it after the price increased.

Perhaps you bought your dream property when the property values were in their worst shape. After the burst of the bubble, property values strongly decreased, and houses and condominiums were available for 40 to 60 percent of their market values. These properties were bargains back then, and if you were smart, you would have bought such a great deal. Today you can sell such a bargain for a very good price and cash in the gain.

If you are thinking about selling your property and getting your money back into your pocket, then this book is a good and easy guide for you to get started. This book will help you to understand what to expect in such a transaction and how best to prepare for it. You certainly want to be successful and to get the best sale price for your property, right?

However, you should not make the mistake of trying to do it alone and your way. You are an alien property owner, and you are subject to the real-estate laws of the foreign country where your property is located. For you as a foreign real-estate owner, there are other rules, laws, and taxes that apply than to a US citizen. Additionally, you have to take the rules and regulations of your home country into consideration when transferring the property-sale proceeds back home into your account.

To avoid the violation of rules and regulations that apply to you, a team of local specialists in the country of your real-estate location—in our case, the United States and, specifically, Florida—is indispensable. This book will show you what you have to consider and which licensed experts you will need.

This book is not a do-it-yourself guide, and it does not replace any advice from an American lawyer or an American tax consultant. Legal and tax advice are not the main focuses of this book, and the reader should not assume such. However, the book can help you identify the open questions and pitfalls in your individual sale transaction and discuss these details with a competent adviser. This will help you avoid sleepless nights and optimize your profits in the property sale.

This book will show you how to find the best decision-making strategy, the best selling time, and the most competent local partners.

Let's begin your project and start reading *Property Sale in a Foreign Country: Global Property Sale—Florida as an Example.*

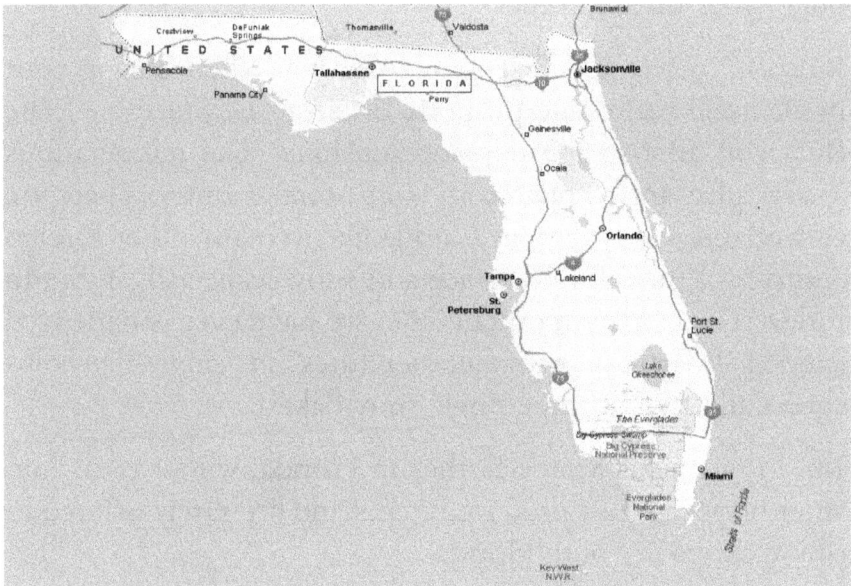

MAKE THE CORRECT PREPARATIONS FOR YOUR PROPERTY SALE IN FLORIDA

In my first book, I showed you a real-estate purchase transaction and the sorts of properties available in foreign countries —however our focus is Florida in the United States. On a virtual level, we have experienced together the journey toward your dream home and walked with you the whole path to your new residence.

On the way to your property ownership, we went the way together and showed you the hurdles and pitfalls. Now we will go the opposite direction and accompany you with your project. The goal of this project is to sell your home at the best possible price.

In order to find the best possible path to sell your property, let us take a step back and look at your motivation when you bought your dream home.

Florida is or was the first choice for you when buying your international real-estate property because the Sunshine State offers you almost 365 days of sunshine. The temperatures are very pleasant compared to your home country. There are less wet and windy days in Florida like in many other foreign countries. You will find no ice and snow, especially in South Florida. The coldest moments that we have ever experienced included hoarfrost with temperatures in single-digit-plus degrees and two or three single snowflakes.

You do not need winter clothes in Florida; winter coats and winter boots are not preferred items and are rarely offered in fashion shops in South Florida.

However, from time to time, you will need an umbrella. It certainly rains, and sometimes these rains are heavy, but they can be compared with a nice shower. The temperatures hardly fall during the rain, and the weather remains pleasantly warm.

Nevertheless, owing a piece of real estate in the state of Florida or another location abroad is not everyone's heaven on earth. Perhaps as a property owner, you miss the change of the seasons, which you will hardly find in Florida. Or homesickness and the longing for friends and family depresses you, and your beautiful dream home loses its charm. You want to go home to your loved ones, friends, and family.

Maybe Florida was your preferred vacation destination because you had small children, and with them you visited many attractions and had fun together. Or you have enjoyed the tropical landscape in the Sunshine State, with its many colorful flowers and the many wild animals that paid your garden a visit. But perhaps this lifestyle has changed, and your property does not fit your lifestyle any longer.

If you bought your property ten years ago, perhaps after the real-estate crash, then the decay of the market values determined your purchase decision. At that time, you could buy high-quality, luxurious homes for little money. Another great advantage at that time was the favorable currency rate of the euro to the US dollar, which was also a big help for the cost-effective acquisition of your dream home.

As a part of the United States, Florida is a very safe state, and the real-estate laws for foreign owners are very beneficial. Due to the public and nearly complete documentation of real-estate properties, you could verify what you were buying.

Personal safety is also very important in Florida. The Sunshine State is the tourist center of the United States, and the government of Florida is doing everything it can to keep it that way.

During your time as a real-estate owner, you certainly have made many friends and met nice neighbors, and you maintain good contacts with each other. Americans are very friendly and welcome every new neighbor, and these good neighborhood connections can now be very useful for your sale plans. For surely you are interested in getting the best price for your home and in making sure that the new owner appreciates your home. These are my experiences as a real-estate broker in Florida.

After this little exercise, we are going to tackle the real-estate project together. In order to determine the correct listing price and your willingness to negotiate in the sale transaction, it is important that you remember your original goal when purchasing the property and also that you keep your future goal in mind. By aligning your ideas, you define your transaction goal and define the best possible strategy for its successful realization.

Let's start with your project.

Do You Own a House or a Condominium?

In order to steer the sale of your dream home in the right direction, you first have to put together some important details. These details include, in addition to the property type—house or condo—information about the location and the condition of the property.

Let's get started. Because you've already owned your property for several years, your sale transaction is considered a resale and not a new construction. As soon as a property owner is registered in the public records, each succeeding property transfer is regarded as a resale. It does not matter if you have never lived in the house yourself.

A new-construction property can only be sold by a developer or a building contractor. Even if you built the property for yourself, this is a resale transaction because you are acting in the capacity of a builder.

Two important details related to the property are when your home was built and what type of construction it is. Is the house a solid construction, or do you own a trailer home?

Yes, they still exist—trailer homes—and they will not disappear so quickly, either. However, such houses are harder to sell than solid houses. The sale price of a mobile home is usually below $50,000, and only a few real-estate professionals are willing to work with such low-priced real-estate properties. The real-estate professionals cannot earn much commission in such a transaction and try to avoid them. Therefore, in many cases, the seller must expect to pay a fixed commission amount that is not based on the selling price of the trailer home.

But even in such a case, you should not go the do-it-yourself path or hire a dubious, unlicensed real-estate person. Details on how to find a competent and licensed real-estate professional can be found in the chapters about the services of real-estate professionals, their knowledge, and their additional trainings and designations.

As already mentioned above, your real-estate sale is a resale transaction, and you as a seller have some disclosure requirements to fulfill, which you should pay attention to. If you do not, you risk the sale transaction being canceled after its completion and the payment of the sale price, because you have kept important information to yourself, and therefore, the buyer feels deceived. Believe me—in a real-estate sale, honesty is the best; otherwise, you end up in court very quickly, and you certainly do not want that. I am speaking from experience and have worked on various problems that could have been avoided if the seller had been open and had informed his real-estate expert properly.

Please also resist the desire to download a standard sale contract from the Internet or use a contract from an unlicensed person, because you are taking an unnecessary and possibly costly risk. A licensed and trustworthy real-estate professional will never provide you with such a contract because the providing professional is liable for your errors in such a contract. On each of these standard contract forms, the real-estate professional is listed and can quickly get into criminal trouble.

Your home certainly has some very beneficial features that can be decisive for the transaction's success and the highest achievable sale price.

Such home features include, among others, a well-preserved structure, well-maintained outdoor amenities, and the location of your property.

The maintenance of the property is, for example, a part of the preservation of the building's structure. When you bought the house, it was either already renovated, or you renovated it. What kind of renovation did you do? Was it only the remodeling of the kitchen and/or bathroom, or did you renovate the windows and doors too, based on the newest building codes? Have you applied for all the necessary building permits, and have these been duly approved by the city?

If you have a boat dock and access to a canal, it is important that you find out the vital details for these features and have them available for the buyer. When was your boat dock built? How deep is the canal? What are the guidelines for the size of the approved boat? What is the distance between the approved boats?

Perhaps you have also built a pool in your backyard after your purchase, and the pool deck is particularly elaborate, built with quality materials. Does the installed pool comply with the newest building codes for pools?

Or maybe you have renovated your patio and then installed an insect-screening structure, or you have an awning in the patio area that your neighbor doesn't have. When did you make these changes?

You will find further details in this field in the following chapters; however, it is very important that you gather as many as possible positive home features. These positive home features are the best ways to stand out from the competition and attract more potential buyers.

It is unnecessary to tell you that all interior and exterior details of your property must be in the best shape possible and spotlessly clean.

The term "location of your property" refers not only to its actual location but also to whether it is in a homeowner community that can influence the sale transaction.

The physical location of your property determines what kind of customers you should seek for your home. For example, if your property is on a canal, the best customer for you will be a boat owner looking for a home with access to open waters. However, a family with children often prefers a home in good condition and with a pool. Such buyers may not be interested in a boat dock.

If your property is located in a homeowner community, it is strongly recommended that you get together all the relevant community documents and provide documentation for the community's maintenance payments. A prospective buyer must be able to review these documents before submitting a corresponding purchase offer for your home. The purchaser has only three days for this review task. Within this period, the purchaser must decide whether to agree with the community rules and regulations and whether he wants to live by these rules and regulations.

Such homeowner-community documents are available not only for house communities but also for condominium complexes. In the condominium communities, these documents are even more important because condominium-community documents are more restrictive for the condo owners and impact their rights on a broader scale.

These regulations often include rules on how much the new property owner must earn to get approval and whether the community has the right of preemption. This right of preemption—also known as the right of first refusal—is intended to prevent the sale of a community property below market value due to a financial default of the present owner. Such a default sale will also affect the market values of the other condo units in the complex. Therefore, the condominium community often has the right to buy this specific property unit directly from the unit owner at market value, and then the community can sell this unit again to get its purchase investment back when it finds a buyer.

The condominium community also has the right to check the financial status of the potential buyer, and therefore, community members conduct a background check. The buyer must have a stable financial status to meet his payment obligation for the maintenance charges. This is to prevent the community from having to pick up this maintenance obligation when the property owner does not pay.

During the real-estate crisis in 2008 and the following years, the default on maintenance charges was the number-one reason for foreclosures in Florida by homeowners' associations. The more property owners become insolvent, the higher the payment pressure became on the other owners. That was not acceptable for the communities.

In this context, it is essential that the homeowners' association inform the selling owner if there are major renovations or modernizations planned in the near future for which the new property owner will have to pay.

Such modernizations can mean repairs or remodeling of interior or exterior features that are used by all condominium owners. These costs are not always covered by the monthly maintenance payments and often require a special payment from the respective owners. A buyer must be informed during the transaction about such upcoming payments.

After this excursion into homeowners' associations, we would like to offer some more information on the sale of an owner-occupied condominium.

The disclosure by a condominium owner about renovations and modernizations is limited to the area inside of the four walls of the condo. In this context, you should emphasize as much as possible the benefits and the condition of your condominium. If you have recently renovated your bathroom, for example, this can increase the interest of buyers and also positively influence the price of the unit.

As already mentioned, renovations and modernization of windows and doors are often established by the homeowner community, and the individual owners of the units have only limited influence over these renovations. However, new windows can also be an excellent sales argument. It depends on the correct representation of these activities.

A highlight that certainly arouses the buyer's interest is accordion hurricane shutters, which not only protect the windows but often also enclose your complete balcony. These shutters are lockable and provide protection not only against the weather but also for your outdoor furniture when you leave it outside.

In the case of an owner-occupied condo, for example, it is also important to know how many parking spaces belong to the condo unit and where these parking spaces are located on the lot. Sometimes a parking spot has its own deed (ownership certificate) that must be transferred separately to the new unit owner.

All this information, as well as the costs for water, power, and maintenance, should be gathered before the listing of the real-estate property. With this preparation, you will prevent delays later in the transaction when it nears closing. You should keep in mind that time is of the essence during the transaction.

Another important detail in regards to condominiums is the different ownership type, which can impact and delay the sale transaction.

There are condominium complexes in which each condominium owner owns the specific named condo. In this case, the owner is registered as the owner for this specific unit in all public records, and he can use this condo as collateral for his real-estate mortgage.

However, there are also condominium complexes that are organized in the form of a cooperative. In this case, all units of the complex belong to the cooperative, and the owner is only a shareholder in the entire condominium complex. If the condo owner needs a loan for the acquisition of such a condo, he cannot use the condo as collateral. He only has ownership of a part of the total cooperative assets and not of a specific condominium. This type of administration is therefore not very popular with residential buyers.

To conclude this chapter, here are some more definitions related to real estate that you should know as a foreign national seller, so there are no misunderstandings with your real-estate expert.

A "villa" in Florida does not mean a large house on a large property lot; it means a one-story attached house with two or three bedrooms and two bathrooms. Such villas usually have no garage and only one or two parking spaces for vehicles in front of the property.

In Florida, the term for a large house on a large lot is "mansion." These mansions are equipped with many luxury and high-end features. Pools and boat docks are usually standard items and nothing special.

A "town house" is a multistory, attached, single-family house. In such a home, there is often a garage on the ground floor, which also contains important home appliances such as a washing machine, dryer, hot-water heater, and air-conditioning unit. The bedrooms and bathrooms are often on the second and third floors.

There is another sort of multistory, attached, single-family home, but the difference from a town house is that such a house is sitting on a lot that belongs to the homeowners' association. Such a property usually has no garage, but only one or two parking spots in front of the building. Based on this detail, such a property is a condominium and not a single-family house.

The counting of the floor begins with the ground floor. The ground floor gets the number one, and the following floor two, three, et cetera. The number zero for the ground floor does not exist.

Based on this information, you are certainly able to categorize your home and prepare yourself for your sale transaction.

Is Your Property in Florida Your Second Home?

To set the sale of your home in the right direction, we first went through some important details in connection with your home. These details are all basic facts related to your property.

In this chapter, we look more closely at the home details in connection with the use of your property; therefore, the question of whether it is a second home or an investment property is important.

If you live and work in Florida, your property will not be the second home for you but the primary residence. Do you think that this question is secondary for you? Then you'd better read the following carefully, because it can cost you money, and the amount of the money is different.

The sale of the primary residence has different tax implications from the sale of a second home or, in this case, an investment property. In this context, it is also important to know whether you are a green card holder or whether you are a US citizen. If neither of these applies for you, then you are an alien or foreign national, and you are subject to the FIRPTA tax code.

Please note that these and the following details on tax terms are merely information in connection with this book and do not constitute tax advice of any kind. For your individual tax implications and questions, it is imperative to consult with an international tax accountant or tax consultant, because the tax laws are adapting constantly. That means that your tax conditions can change from one day to the other.

FIRPTA means Foreign Investment in Real Property Tax A ct. This taxation stipulates that each foreign real-estate seller has to pay 10 percent tax, calculated on the selling price of the property, if the buyer uses this property as his primary residence.

In February 2016, the rate for this tax regulation was changed. Under certain circumstances, this tax can either be avoided, or you must pay even more than 10 percent—details to follow. With a selling price of less than $300,000, this tax can be avoided if the purchaser uses the property as his or her primary residence.

However, this exemption is not practiced by the title companies due to the strict criminal and liability measures in the United States in relation to the tax code, and you must be prepared to pay this 10 percent tax in the first place. But you must file your US income tax in the year following the property sale with the Internal Revenue Service (IRS) and claim this tax amount.

This task is a little bit complicated, and if you need assistance, require a competent tax consultant, or have questions regarding where to start, please send an e-mail to the e-mail address at the end of this book. We can certainly help you.

If the purchase price is greater than $300,000 and less than $1 million, then the 10 percent will be charged and cannot be refunded even when you file a tax return with the IRS. For a real-estate sale price above $1 million, the FIRPTA tax increases to 15 percent, and it does not matter whether the buyer uses the purchased property as his or her primary residence.

This FIRPTA tax applies only to foreign nationals. For US citizens, the sale of a primary residence is tax-free within certain limits. A US citizen can sell his or her house without paying taxes every five years if the owner has lived in the property for at least twenty-four months and if the sale gain of the real-estate property does not exceed the tax-free limits.

If you consider your property to be an investment and you have earned rental income from it, then you should for sure meet with a tax account for a discussion of your individual situation. In such a case, different regulations apply than from if you use the property by yourself. If you have an investment property and buy a new one, there are also special rules to consider so that you can reduce or delay your tax liability.

In addition to tax considerations, the maintenance costs, such as gardening and pool maintenance, must be taken into account, as well as the repairs of household appliances when the property has been used as a second home. Such costs occurring during the ownership of the property shall be taken into account when determining the taxable sale profit. Perhaps you can deduct some of these costs and reduce your sale profit.

The above-mentioned costs also inform the buyer which costs to expect when purchasing the property. A very important item in this context is the air-conditioning. Due to the climatic conditions, the air-conditioning unit must be running throughout the year, and that causes costs that may be of interest to the buyer, especially when the buyer intends to use the property as a second home. Please keep this information handy for your potential buyer, who will be thankful for it.

Another important point is that you will rarely service your second home in the same way as your primary residence. This can lead to much renovation effort for the buyer, and that can mean a price reduction in favor to the purchaser. Make a list of all things that a buyer might not accept, and calculate the costs. You can decide later if you want to spend money on this and fix these deficiencies or rather reduce the purchase price. At this stage, this decision is not yet relevant, and gathering the information is only a preparation for you.

These are just a few hints that you should consider in advance before talking to a real-estate specialist and getting ready for the listing to be posted on the market. When you have all details ready, you are perfectly prepared for the first customer who will pay you the best possible price for your property.

What Is Your Motivation for Your Property Sale?

We have taken the first two steps on your way to a successful sale of your property.

We started with the gathering of all relevant real-estate details of your property, and we made the first evaluation of tax and sale-price considerations. Now it is time to look more closely at your sale motivation. The simple decision to "just get rid of the property" is not always the best, and you may leave lots of money on the table.

To make your real-estate sale a success, the right timing for your property sale is enormously important. Not every time is equally good for the highest possible sale price.

There are particular time periods in Florida where a property attracts more prospects and is sold faster than others. The reason for this is not only the general property-market situation but also the available buyer pool for your property.

Florida is a vacation hot spot and tropical paradise. The main vacation time is from the end of the hurricane season—November—to Easter. In this time period, there are more potential buyers in Florida from all over the world than at any other time. These buyers are often looking for a second home or an investment property. When you decide to sell, this is the best time to do it.

Besides this consideration, it is also important to realize what your personal motivations are for the real-estate sale and how quickly you want to close the transaction. On these bases, your real-estate professional has to determine the listing price and to conduct the succeeding sale negotiations with potential buyers.

With a clear objective in terms of sale price and a time frame for the transaction, you and your real-estate professional can prepare and conclude a very lucrative property transaction together.

Let us now look a little bit more at some of your possible motivations and evaluate their impact on the success of a transaction.

You want a bigger new home

Maybe you currently own a condominium, and now you want to buy a house. Or your present home has only two bedrooms and one bathroom, and now your family is growing with another child, and you need more space. Or your mother or father cannot live alone anymore, and you want to take your parent in with you.

If your family grows, it is important to consider who your new family member will be. If the new family member is a child, there are different requirements to consider for the new property than if the new member is your parent.

In case a child is the reason for a bigger home, your next home can be a multistory house or town house. If, on the other hand, your parent moves in, it is usually more convenient when there are no stairs to climb to get to his or her bedroom.

Whatever your next property looks like, you will have to put more money on the table for the purchase and, if necessary, apply for a higher mortgage.

If you do not want to spend more money than you spent on your present home, you will need to look for a property that needs to be renovated or modernized. In such a case, you will use so-called sweat money or muscle strength to cover the purchase-price difference, and you will do many renovating tasks yourself.

Under this premise, the goal for your listing price is to get as much money as possible. To achieve this goal, your present property must be in excellent condition so that the potential purchaser will not find any argument for a sale-price reduction.

It is also important that the desired sale price is calculated in such a way that it is within the neighborhood's property market values. Each listing price (the desired sale price, presented on the Internet marketing web pages) that is not within the range of the neighborhood market values will affect the transaction positively or negatively, depending on the condition of your property.

To find the best listing price for your property, within the neighborhood price range, you and your real-estate expert should sit together and evaluate all known facts. Details for this area can be found in the chapter entitled "You wish to liquidate an investment property."

You want a smaller home

Your reason for selling your property and purchasing a different one can also be that your child or children have moved out and have families of their own. In such a case, the current Florida real-estate market (as of 2017) can be a great opportunity for you.

If, for example, you have a house with more than two bedrooms, and now you need less living space, you can either buy a smaller house or a condominium. There is a good selection of new constructions and resale properties available that will meet your expectations.

When you stick with a house, you will have to continue to care for the maintenance of the outdoor features, which means you must cut the lawn and hedges, and that may be too exhausting or too boring for you.

In such a case, a condominium is certainly the better solution for you. With a condominium, the homeowners' association takes care of the outdoor amenities and features, and you can comfortably lift your feet on a footstool and enjoy life.

If you opt for a condominium and you are older than fifty-five, then a unit in one of the fifty-five-plus communities may be interesting. These condominiums are often cheaper than the units in communities without age regulations.

These fifty-five-plus communities are usually very well maintained and offer everything you could wish for: tennis courts, golf ranges, swimming pools, and community activities. In addition, there is often a private or municipal bus shuttle service that will take you quickly and easily to the nearest shopping mall.

As mentioned above, these condominiums are cheaper, and if you sell your current property at a profit, you will have a nice cash amount to make your new property nice and attractive and additionally save some money for emergencies.

In such a sale situation, you can limit the renovation efforts of your property to cosmetic embellishments, such as painting the walls or installing a modern faucet. Perhaps a thorough cleaning is sufficient because your home is in good condition.

In this situation, you are more flexible in the price negotiations and thus can speed up the sale transaction. Details on the right pricing can be found in one of the following chapters.

You are a foreign national, and you are no longer interested in living in Florida because your attitude toward the political environment has changed

Do you think this is an invented reason? I thought so too, but every political decision has an impact on the purchase and sale of real-estate properties. This shows the behavior of the customers.

One thing is certain—Florida is part of the United States, and it is politically stable, and your homeownership rights are very secure. Political change will not change that.

Due to the economic and political situations of Florida, all signs of development are currently positive in the economic sectors. Property prices are rising, new constructions are shooting out of the ground everywhere, and the purchase demand is growing too. In areas where not enough new construction units are available, resale properties are an excellent substitute.

Therefore, this reason is not a good argument for a sale decision. Your personal motivation and the positive real-estate market must be the only decision criteria.

You need to relocate because you have a new job or your financial situation has changed

This is a very valid reason for selling your property, and it can happen to anyone, regardless of whether the seller is a foreign national or US citizen.

A job change, for example, can occur when your employer goes out of business, or your job and services are no longer needed, or the overall economic situation in the industry has deteriorated, or any other thinkable reason. The result is that you lose your job, and there is no option to avoid it.

Perhaps you do not like your job anymore, and you terminate your job engagement for a better option in another city. Or perhaps you become sick and can no longer fulfill your existing job requirements.

Whatever happens in such a situation, the fact is that your financial base is changing. Because of this financial base change, your own economic environment and the criteria for your property are changing too. A job change often involves a property sale at your old location and a purchase at your new job location. Meanwhile, a change of financial situation due to illness or job loss will often force you to move into a cheaper or smaller home.

In addition to personal reasons, mortgage terms also need your attention. Especially in case of a financial crisis due to job loss or illness, a "short sale" may be the only option for you to protect yourself and your credit score. Such a transaction is complicated and time consuming.

A well-trained real-estate specialist for short sales is the best choice for your property sale. You can find out more about this specialty in real estate in the chapters about the education of real-estate professionals, or you can contact us by e-mail. Please use the e-mail at the end of this book, and we will help you to find such a specialist at your location.

You are facing a divorce, and your home is part of the divorce settlement

This reason is similar to the above reason and should not to be underestimated in its explosiveness. If, in this context, mistakes are made during the divorce process, then the sale of the property can be significantly delayed at best and impossible at worst.

Here are a few multiyear experiences in this area that will show you why it is extremely important to complete all the necessary steps in this process.

We received a request from a customer to sell his property; our first look in such a case is at the tax data of the city in which the property is located. When inspecting the public records, we discovered that the seller who had contacted us was not the only owner. Besides the seller, his ex-wife was still registered in the records.

In response to our questions, the customer indicated that the divorce had been concluded years ago and that the divorce verdict was legally binding and entered into at court. Our further research confirmed that this only partially true. The ex-wife had been released from the loan liability during the divorce negotiation, and in connection with the mortgage only, our customer was the owner of the property. However, the divorced couple forgot to correct and transcribe the public records of the real-estate property, so these records still showed the wrong information.

Because of this failure, the ex-wife was still co-owner of the property, and therefore, she had to agree not only to sell the property but also to participate actively in the process. However, the ex-wife was not interested in cooperating, and finally the property went into foreclosure, with negative consequences for both the ex-wife and the property owner.

If you want to sell your property in a similar situation, be sure to consult a lawyer and go through all the necessary steps before you put your property on the market.

In order to spice up the whole matter, let us make clear that the above-described case can occur during an ongoing divorce in a modified form. It is particularly complicated when the married persons are from different countries—for example, an American and a European. In such a case, not only the real-estate laws but also the immigration regulations can be challenges. Without a competent lawyer, every step will be very slow and complicated.

In such a situation, it is not easy to determine the best possible listing price, and every party—sellers and real-estate professional—has to give his or her best. It requires joint efforts from all parties to complete such a sale transaction successfully.

It should be in the interest of all property owners to obtain the best sale price and to ensure that the transaction closes as fast as possible. The sale proceeds can be shared quickly among the homeowners, and each real-estate owner can then pursue his or her individual goal.

Perhaps you will marry again and need a new property. We are happy to offer you our many years of experience in the business, either for your sale or purchase of a property.

One or all property owners have died

Already, a property sale in connection with a divorce is a challenge, but when the sad event has occurred that one or all of the property owners has passed away, then a property sale becomes really difficult. The peculiar challenge in this context arises when the owners are foreign nationals—aliens or non-US citizens.

In such a case, the assistance of a US lawyer is mandatory—not for the property sale but because of the inheritance problem. When a real-estate property belongs to a heritage, then legal proceedings are required for the transfer of the property. The following description is only meant to understand the issue and does not constitute legal advice.

Let's say you are married and own a property together with your wife, your husband, or your life partner, whatever it is. Now one of the real-estate owners dies, and there is no will. In this case, the surviving owner becomes immediately the sole owner of the property and can correct the public records immediately, without further court proceedings. A legal inheritance regulation—like in Germany, where the children inherit a part of the whole inheritance—does not exist in Florida.

However, if there is a will or if the surviving spouse dies too, then an attorney must file a probate case in the court of law. This filing must be done in each state where the deceased had assets. In the United States or Florida, for example, the heir will need a judicial certificate from the court to transfer a real-estate property into his or her name. Other states may have additional requirements in a probate case.

When you have the necessary court papers for the correction of the public record in connection with the real-estate property, then you can hire your real-estate specialist and start the marketing for your home.

If one of the homeowners dies during an ongoing real-estate transaction and there already exists a binding sale contract for the property, the heirs are bound to this existing contract. The heirs have no option to terminate this contract, and they have to complete the transaction to the bitter end.

In this context, that means this: A couple has listed their property on the market, and a buyer has already made an offer. The sellers/homeowners have also signed this offer. Now this offer becomes an executed contract (details are following in one of the next chapters), and the surviving homeowner in the contract has to fulfill this contract. The death of the spouse and homeowner does not kill a signed sale contract for a property. The Florida real-estate laws apply in this situation, and not the property laws of your home country, when you are an alien in Florida.

Another inconvenience in this connection is the inheritance tax, which does not exist in Florida, but on the federal level of the United States. For an inheriting US citizen, the tax-free limit for a heritage is anything above $1 million, but for a foreign national, the tax-free inheritance limit is $60,000, regardless of the relationship between the heirs and the deceased person.

In order to avoid or to reduce the aforementioned inheritance tax, there is the option to put a real-estate property into a trust in favor of a beneficiary. When the property is part of a trust, there is no death; only the beneficiary can die, and the inheritance tax is thereby positively influenced. How and in what form such a trust has to be designed to get the most benefit, you will need to discuss with your American tax consultant and your lawyer. Details on this matter are regarded as tax and legal advice, and such advice may only be given by licensed professionals in those fields. But one thing is certain—such a trust must be established in a timely manner before the death happens. When one of the owners is already dead, it is too late.

Besides the inheritance tax, the already-mentioned FIRPTA tax is also payable. We have already mentioned the FIRPTA tax rate in one of the preceding chapters, and the personal income tax rate applies to the inheritance tax. However, there may be changes in the future because tax laws are constantly changing and adapting, as in each other country.

You wish to liquidate an investment property

Let us now turn to the reason that is mainly interesting for property investors and foreign real-estate professionals: a property sale to liquidate the capital invested in the property and the reinvestment in a different business goal.

In this context, it is important to consider the entire period of ownership and, in particular, to examine the purchase price in the past, today's market price, and, if necessary, the currency-conversion rate.

The currency conversion is especially important when you want to sell the property and transfer the money from the United States back to your home country.

The money transfer from the States is easy to do, but it is convenient to observe the daily exchange rates of the US dollar into your home country's currency and wait for a favorable rate to get the most out of your advantageous sale transaction.

If this is too difficult for you, we can provide you with prestigious business contacts that can assist you with this matter in a comfortable and lucrative way. If you are interested in these trustworthy and experienced partners, please send us an e-mail at the address at the end of the book.

Let us now carry out a small calculation example in order to examine the above-mentioned information. This examination will make your sale decision much easier.

We will assume that you bought your property as a bank foreclosure during the downturn of the real-estate market in the United States in 2008.

In September 2008, the currency-conversion rate was €1 .00 to $1.41, and in 2014 the exchange rate was €1.00 to $1.26. This ratio changed to €1.00 to $1.12 by September 2016. This means you needed a lot fewer euros for the purchase, and because of the increase of the property value and the stronger US dollar exchange rate, you will realize a nice profit from your sale.

The chosen property in our example is one block from the federal highway (which runs close to the east coast of Florida, to Key West). The exterior construction is massively built and well maintained and is located on an oversized lot.

Please look also at this calculation for a better understanding:

Year	Purchase Price in USD	Currency Rate	Euro Amount
2005	220,000.00	0	0.00
2008	90,000.00	1.41	63,829.79
2014	128,100.00	1.26	101,666.67
Gain			*37,836.88*
2016	174,931.00	1.12	156,188.39
Gain			*92,358.61*

As you can see, the development of the real-estate market and the currency conversion has been very beneficial for property owners. If you spent around €63,830 in 2008, you would get back €156,189 in 2016. This corresponds to a profit of €92,358, whereby renovation, maintenance, and taxes were not taken into account.

Which Options Do You Have When Changing a Property?

This book focuses on selling a property in Florida. However, a sale is not always the best option for you, and there may be another one that better fits your needs.

In the preceding chapters, we put together a few reasons for a sale and examined their effects and consequences on your sale transaction. Any reason that you consider can have a different positive outcome on the sale result.

Especially in the previous chapter, we have considered the option of liquidation, and based on the currently very narrow property market in Florida—short inventory, increasing demand, and rising home prices—it may be useful to wait a bit longer and observe the market movements closely.

If you have not yet decided, take some more time and think about the financial goals you want to achieve with the money in the future.

Do you want to buy a new property with the received sale price?

Do you want to invest the money in the stock market?

Do you need the money for an urgent purchase, or are you going into retirement and want to enjoy the fruits of your hard work?

If these questions are not yet answered, then you should consider both available options and find out which one fits best for you:

Sell or rent?

Sell the property

Let us first look a little bit closer at the option of selling the property. What was your motivation when you bought the property in Florida?

Florida is the Sunshine State, and the sun shines here all year long. The temperatures are pleasantly warm, and rain falls only rarely. And if it rains, then this rain is often heavy and of short duration, followed by sunshine.

You do not need winter clothing here. No winter coat, no scarf, and no cap necessary, unless you leave Florida during the wintertime, going northward or to Europe. For cooler days, a long-sleeved blouse, a light cardigan or sweater, a pair of socks and sneakers—that is all you need. On warm days, flip-flops, short pants, and a shirt are the way to go.

There is always something to undertake here. You can go to the beach and enjoy the sand, sun, water, and wind. Or you can go deep-sea fishing like Hemingway did or dive for treasures like Mel Fisher and have a good time.

Other ways to entertain yourself include the many amusement parks, museums, theaters, and casinos. Do not forget the Caribbean cruises that start from Miami and Fort Lauderdale and take you back into the times of pirates and adventurers.

When you sell your Florida home to leave the state, then you will leave all these entertainments behind you. Perhaps you have enjoyed all the above benefits long enough, and your senses are now looking for new adventures at different destinations far away from Florida. If so, then the property sale is certainly the right option for you.

Another financial advantage of selling is that you eliminate the costs you have to pay as a property owner when you sell.

Such costs include, for example, gardening, lawn mowing, and pool maintenance, because the trees and bushes grow pretty well and quick in the Florida climate, and the water of the pool becomes quickly green. To avoid this, you have to mow the lawn every week, cut the shrubbery regularly, and clean the pool; otherwise it will become a filthy breeding ground for mosquitoes.

The air-conditioning system in your home must be constantly running so that the interior of your property does not get mold damage in the subtropical climate. This results in power costs, which are eliminated when you sell your home.

If you have a condominium, you do not need to take care of the exterior features of your property because the homeowners' association takes care of that, but you have to pay monthly maintenance fees for these tasks.

Other costs are the homeowners' insurance and the annual property tax, which are significant cost items for every homeowner. The amount of these costs depends on the location and how big and luxurious your property is.

When you sell your property, you have to consider the real-estate professional's commission as well as the procession costs that are involved in the sale transaction. A rough cost estimate is about 9 percent of the sale price. The FIRPTA tax is not included in these costs because this tax will be refunded from the tax authority based on the sale price and your residency status.

As already mentioned in one of the above chapters, a 10 percent FIRPTA tax will be due on a property sale if you are a foreign national. However, you can claim this tax amount in the year following the sale when you file a tax return with the US Internal Revenue Service (IRS).

After looking at these details, consider carefully the time when you want to sell your property. This question is particularly important because not every time is equally good for your property sale.

As you certainly know, Florida is a vacation destination, and it attracts millions of tourists each year, but these visitors do not come evenly throughout the year.

The high season for tourists is from about the end of October until mid-April; in this range, the hurricane season is about to end, and the temperatures become somewhat more moderate. In this period, significantly more potential buyers become available for your property in Florida. As you know, the more interested purchasers are on the market, the greater the chances are to sell the property quickly, easily, and at a high price.

The higher the sale price for your property, the more money you can spend on your new goals. However, this principle can only be implemented with a competent real-estate expert. He or she knows the local real-estate market, is familiar with the best marketing methods and tools, and has the best buyer pool at hand.

The do-it-yourself way is not recommended due to the complexity of the property transaction—and you will not save the commission for the real-estate professional either. If a buyer comes with his own agent, you will indirectly pay this agent. For more information on this topic, please see the section entitled "Sale transaction as 'for sale by owner' (FSBO)."

Rent the property

Let us now consider the option of renting your property, which can be a better option under certain circumstances than the sale.

In the case that you leave your property only for professional reasons and intend to return in the future, a sale does not make sense. You will have doubled the costs—paying once for your property sale today and another time when you buy a new property upon your return.

However, and this has to be considered, the fixed costs such as the annual property tax, the property insurance, as well as the maintenance and repair expenses will remain unchanged. These costs must be covered by the rental payments from the tenants.

Before you put your property on the market as a rental home, you should check with your city to see if there are requirements to consider when renting your property. For example, the building department of a city often requires that rental properties are equipped with smoke detectors in all rooms and fire extinguishers in the house. These are the minimum requirements, and there may be more that are also checked by the building inspector and the fire inspector. You also need to register with the city as a landlord.

You will need a real-estate professional who takes care of your property and its maintenance during your absence. You can also restrict the job of the agent to the marketing of your rental property, but in that case, you are responsible for collecting the rental payments and ensuring maintenance and repairs of your property, even when you are not local. If this is desirable to you, keep in mind that the workload depends on your time—and your ability to respond to tenants' requests and to take care of rental issues within twenty-four hours, seven days a week.

Let us now look at the details for a rental property and the calculation of the rent. If you rent a single-family house, the rental cost and rental payment are different than if you rent a condominium. You cannot apply the leasing rules of your home country to Florida, which has different regulations.

In your home country, there may be something called rent, which means the rental payment only for the dwelling, and costs like cable, rent security, water, trash, et cetera, are added into to the monthly lease payment. The tenant pays the total sum of both as a monthly rent amount. In the United States, this is handled differently.

Let us first examine the case of renting a single-family house. For such a rental, we assume a long-term lease (at least one year). Vacation rentals are more complicated and are explained separately.

When you as the owner calculate the monthly rent payments, there are no limitations to consider other than the market rule of supply and demand. That means you can ask for any rent amount you want, but it depends if you will get it. There is no government agency or any other consumer authority that checks whether your rent is too high. However, if your rent is above the common rental rate, then you will not find a tenant for your unit, and you will not generate income.

Another important point is what kinds of services are included in the monthly rental payment. Landlords often offer as a part of the rental payment free Internet and cable access. However, there is no separate billing made when the tenant leaves the premises or when the tenant stays longer than one year.

Power, water, and sewer costs are often not part of the monthly rental and are usually paid by the tenant himself. The tenant choses the providers and pays the monthly invoice directly to the service provider. The consumption invoice is calculated on a monthly base and sent to the tenant for payment. The homeowner/landlord gets usually a copy of the bill.

For the maintenance of the exterior and the pool, you as the landlord should hire a service provider who takes care of these tasks. This ensures that the necessary activities are done properly and in a timely matter. In case the city files a complaint against you based on failure to comply with a city regulation, then you can take recourse to the service provider.

If you entrust your tenant with these tasks, it could happen that the tenant does not do everything in the way you both have agreed on or that the tenant injures himself in performing these tasks. In such a case, you are liable for the costs incurred by the tenant. When you as the landlord get a complaint from the city because the lawn was not mowed in time, then you, the owner of the property, are responsible for the fine and not your tenant. It is hard to get such fines refunded from a tenant.

When renting a condominium, there are a few deviations to be considered. Let us see what that means to you.

Before you rent your condo unit, please check your homeowner and condominium documents. These documents may have some rental restrictions, perhaps limiting the frequency of possible rentals throughout the year, or stipulating that the rental period last at least thirty days or longer.

In the case of an owner-occupied condominium, the costs for cable service, water, and sewer as well as for the maintenance of the exterior facilities are included in the monthly homeowners' association fee. Internet access is usually not part of this monthly payment, but you can allow your tenant to use your Internet access, if you have it. The tenant is in this case not liable for the costs, and you must include the costs in your rental payment. Again, there is no separate billing or charge when your tenant leaves, as may be common in your home country.

A short-term rental property or condominium is usually rented furnished, while long-term rentals are offered unfurnished. But you always should charge a security to cover your damages that may occur during the lease period.

Another special feature in connection with rentals is the homeowners' association. It has to agree to your rental request. Any potential tenant must go through a review process with the homeowners' association and the homeowners' board. This process is called application, and without a successful application and the approval from the homeowners' board, your tenant is not allowed to move in.

For the application process, your future tenant has to pay a fee, and with this fee, the costs for the background check of your tenant are paid. During the application process, various databases are checked to determine whether there is a criminal record available, whether there exists a drug dependency, whether there are any financial or payment problems known, and much more.

The intention of these background checks is the protection of the rental community. Everyone who lives in the rental complex should feel safe. These checks are subject to the strict limits of the Fair Housing Act of the United States.

This federal law applies equally to all fifty states. Any infringement is a violation of a federal law and is therefore pursued by a national agency, the United States Department of Housing and Urban Development. More details on this topic can be found in the chapter about fair housing further down in this book.

If the background check of the potential tenant does not produce a result, then your tenant will be invited to a meeting with the homeowners' board to introduce him- or herself. The purpose of this meeting is to get a personal impression of your tenant and discuss with him or her any questions about the house rules and regulations. At the end of this meeting, the homeowners' board gives either an approval or a denial to the tenant. When your tenant is denied, then you must look for a different tenant. As the rental unit owner, you have no right and no option to fight this decision.

All these details regarding costs and application processes apply not only to long-term tenants with rental periods of six months and longer but also to short-term tenants in vacation apartments, if the rental units are located in an association complex.

The difference between a short-term rental and a long-term rental is that in a short-term rental, all costs—power, cable, Internet, water, sewer, and trash—are included in the rental payment. In this case, you as the landlord are the responsible payer for these services and not your tenant.

Besides the above information, you need to check with your city administration to find out if there is a tourist tax to pay for short-term rentals. This is mostly the case when your property is close to tourist centers. These tax rates vary from county to county, and therefore, we will not go deeper into this topic. You have to find out from your city or municipality administration how much this local tourist tax is.

Rental payments are income, and you have to declare this income and pay income tax for it. In Florida there is no state income tax, but there is a federal income tax for this income. Please consult with your tax adviser regarding which costs you can deduct from this income to reduce your taxes due. Details on this topic are beyond the scope of this book and will not be discussed any further.

The following is a sample calculation for a short-term rental unit (fictitious data):

Furnished beachfront condominium

Monthly rent: $3,600

Attention! You have to check your condominium and association documents for the allowed rental period and the frequency of such lease agreements—also see the information above.

Rental income (3 x $3,600.00)	$10,800.00
Unit empty 10 percent (not considered here)	$0.00
Effective income	$10,800.00
Annual expenses (estimated 40 percent): repairs, insurance, taxes, et cetera	$4,320.00
Operational income (same as net income)	$6,480.00
Depreciation (not considered with short-term rental)	$0.00
Income before tax (tax advice and calculation of deductible expenses from your accountant)	$6,480.00

The Decision Is Made—Sale of the Property

In the previous chapters, we examined your motivation and the reasons for the sale of your property in many ways and from many angles.

At this point, your decision should be made, and this decision is now the goal you are working toward. We will go in the direction of a sale. The successful sale transaction is now our project goal.

After the target definition, we start with the next step. You will need some assistance with your sale tasks so that your project achieves for you the most profitable results.

The next step is to decide which path you want to take: go with a real-estate professional (strongly recommended) or do it yourself. The latter option is particularly associated with great risks and very intensive work, as we will see. Additionally, this option is usually more expensive. Why will be explained in the chapter "Sale transaction as 'for sale by owner' (FSBO)."

Sale transaction with the assistance of a real-estate professional

Let us now explore the sale option in which a real-estate professional is assisting you. In Germany, such professionals are comparable to a makler—that means "broker"—but the job regulations in the United States are not comparable with those in Germany.

The most significant point is that the role of these professionals is much broader in the United States than in Germany. The professional in the United States not only markets the property but also manages the entire real-estate transaction from start to finish.

You get around-the-clock service, and you do not have to worry about the individual steps within the transaction, because your expert takes care of that. A detailed description of these activities is found in the chapter on the tasks of a real-estate specialist.

For all the tasks and activities that your personal broker accepts, you pay him a commission. This commission is due when your sale transaction closes successfully, and you have received your sale proceeds.

The commission is calculated on the basis of the selling price, and currently the commission rate is 6 to 7 percent in South Florida. This is the common percentage for that region, but it can be different in each other county.

Sale transaction as "for sale by owner" (FSBO)

With this option, you do not have your own real-estate professional to help you with all important tasks and assist you with all questions.

In such a transaction, you are your own agent, and you are responsible for all necessary activities, dates, and negotiations with the buyer.

You have to make your property appealing for potential buyers yourself and present it on the Internet. You do not have any far-reaching marketing tools like real-estate experts have to market your property optimally. You carry all the risk for problems occurring during the sale transaction. Mistakes that you make and do not solve properly can lead to costly court proceedings.

Perhaps you want to go for this option because you want to save on the commission for the real-estate expert. Unfortunately, you have fallen subject to a misunderstanding. Just because you do not have your own agent with an exclusive contract with you to market the property, that does not mean that the buyer doesn't have an agent.

The buyer's real-estate professional has a right to payment, and even if the buyer is responsible for this payment, he will include this payment in the offered purchase price for your property. In this case, you still pay the commission indirectly.

On the other hand, the buyer's agent can also ignore your property when putting together a selection of homes and presenting the property list to the customer. The agent is not obligated to market your property if he or she does not get paid for the showing or if he or she has to negotiate with you for the commission.

In such a case, you will be much more dependent on the support of a real-estate attorney. The fees for the attorney's real-estate services are much higher than you expect. Also, the attorney will only handle the legal matters and will not market your property. The property marketing is exclusively in your hands.

This sale option is not recommended due to the associated risks and the related tasks of the transaction.

Which Tasks Will Your Real-Estate Professional Perform in a Sale Transaction?

In order to explain this topic focused on Florida, it is necessary to examine the real-estate sale transaction in your home country and clarify this process first. As an example, we will select a property sale and real-estate-marketing methods in Germany.

Usually a real-estate owner tries to sell a property by himself because a real-estate broker costs money, and who wants to spend money on someone who may be less competent than himself? Or so go your thoughts. Whether this attitude is actually successful we will not discuss here. You can, of course, advertise your property on your own in daily newspapers and on Internet portals and try to find the best buyer for your home or condominium. But that can be tough.

On the many real-estate web pages on the Internet, you will also find tons of comparable properties that will give you a clue for your selling price. Or you can ask in your neighborhood which house was recently sold, during the last weeks, and at what price.

In order to get a better and more independent overview of the common real-estate prices in your location, you can also request a market report of your region from the local land registry for a small fee.

In this market-value report, you will also find a description on the condition and the valuation criteria of the properties that were used to determine the published market value.

To calculate the income-producing value of your property, you will need to research on the Internet and in the daily newspapers and find out the average lease payments in your area for similar properties like yours.

With these market data, however, you get only a small insight into the local real-estate market because not all property owners offer their properties on the portals and in the digital media. The quality of the available data depends on the willingness of the property owners to present these data and keep them up to date.

Another option to determine your property value is to use available calculation tools on the Internet. However, these tools cannot include local specialties. The tools only use data that are provided and fed into databases, but details such as popularity of a particular home location are often not taken into consideration by the calculation system. Even recent changes in real-estate values, like environmental issues, are rarely included in these tools. There are simply not enough connected real-estate databases on the Internet that offer such details and allow direct statistical evaluation of real-estate constructions, as is possible in the United States, for example.

If you hire a real-estate specialist in your home country to market your property, this expert can surely create an appropriate market-valuation report, because he has more data sources available than you do.

When you decide to market your property together with a real-estate specialist, you should definitely discuss with him what tasks and activities he will work on and whether you need to pay for them. It is particularly important to note how and where the real-estate professional is marketed. According to the current information, for example, there is no central database for real estate in Germany, and every real-estate office has its own marketing methods, so it is not known how many potential customers will see your property.

Often there is no regulation defined for payment of real-estate services, and therefore, you have to negotiate these costs with your real-estate professional, along with who will pay. The commission is approximately 6 percent plus VAT, and this amount may be paid either by the buyer or by the seller or jointly by both parties.

If you hire a real-estate specialist to market your property as a rental, then you have to know a few special rules. But these rules are not the focus of this book and will not be discussed here.

On the European real-estate portals, already-sold real-estate properties are often still offered, and the presented properties are not always represented by the advertising brokerage offices, because there are no strict regulations in this regards. Each brokerage office can publish properties with the intention to get leads for potential buyers and tenants, even without an exclusive marketing agreement. This can also happen with real-estate properties that are located not in your home country, but in a foreign country. In the United States, the marketing of a property is only allowed when the real-estate professional has an exclusive listing contract.

It can happen that the advertised properties are no longer on the market, but they are still visible on the real-estate portal because the advertisement period has not yet expired or the advertiser has not deleted the ad.

The details of the listing are not always accurate and up to date because these ads must be maintained manually, and not every property owner and broker takes the time and care to keep his or her listings current and to correct mistakes or status changes.

These examples show that Internet property offers are heavily dependent on the advertising owner or brokerage office and the monthly ad budget for the property. Therefore, only a limited selection of all available properties in the local real-estate market is presented and visible on the Internet.

This presented information is based on our own experience and research on the Internet. The brokers who have marketed and tried to sell our own properties have always gotten the correct data and price adjustments from us, but neither the brokers nor their offices have corrected their sales brochures, nor have they ever presented us with a willing and financially capable buyer.

In the case of foreign real-estate properties offered on web portals in Europe, caution is necessary because these properties are often requested from American or other foreign broker colleagues as samples. Therefore, these houses and condos are usually only offered to attract potential customers. If you request more information on these dream homes, you often hear that this property was just sold or is at least under contract. The real-estate broker in Europe has "forgotten" to take this offer down, or the broker continues to use it to attract customers for his own properties.

The market in the United States is much faster and more dynamic than in the German-speaking or European region, and the real-estate inventory is more comprehensively and extensively represented on the Internet. The above-mentioned problems with real-estate data don't exist, or at least are less common, in the US real-estate market because the licensed real-estate professionals work with connected databases.

Another significant difference between a German and an American real-estate broker is the legal part. A German real-estate broker can open his business right away, and the agent only needs a trade license from the local municipality. A certificate of proficiency or an exam for the profession that shows his knowledge is not necessary. Experience and expertise are also not required by law.

However, there is an opportunity to work together with real-estate professionals in other countries and earn money on a global level. In order to facilitate this cooperation, there are cooperation agreements in place with real-estate associations in these other countries. This means that real-estate professionals from your home country can easily and smoothly work with real-estate brokers in the United States. Non-US real-estate experts cannot sell or be parties in a binding real-estate transaction because they lack the necessary US license for the real-estate business. But they can earn a referral fee from a US Realtor when the transaction they worked on together closes. Details on this matter are explained in the following chapter.

Which Professional Requirements Are Mandatory for American Real-Estate Professionals?

The professional profile and work scope of a real-estate specialist are totally different and more diversely organized in the United States than in many other countries. The following description shows the most significant differences compared to a real-estate professional in the German-speaking or European region.

In order to be able to conduct services as a real-estate professional in the United States, the agent first has to complete his or her study successfully in the industry field in English.

As soon as the agent has completed the study program successfully, he or she can apply for the state examination. In the examination process, the agent has to provide fingerprints and personal information about his or her business life so far. This information is checked against several databases before the agent is allowed to take the state exam. When an agent has, for example, a record for drunk driving, this needs to be revealed, because otherwise this matter can become a problem for the agent's new profession in the real-estate business.

When the background check is completed, the approved person is granted permission to take the exam. This exam is very challenging and includes not only job-related topics but also accompanying occupational matters such as tax law, contract law, and financing options. The new agent has to understand the overall context of these different topics within the real-estate transaction. The passing rate of the real-estate students is low, and approximately 80 percent fall through. A repetition of this exam is only possible once without repeating the entire study program.

After the successful completion of the exam, the new real-estate agent receives his or her professional license from the governor of Florida. This license is valid for two years and has to be renewed every two years.

The license renewal is only granted when the necessary supplementary studies are successfully completed and the state has proof of these studies in the system. If these requirements are not met, the license expires, and conducting real-estate services becomes illegal for this agent or broker. The active real-estate license is a seal for quality, and you as a seller should always check the license.

What Does "Sales Agent" or "Sales Associate" Mean in Florida?

During the first two years after passing the exam, the sales agent (that is the official name) has to work as a freelancer in a real-estate office, a brokerage, under the supervision of the office broker.

Within this period, the new sales agent has to go to further training sessions to deepen his or her knowledge, and these education sessions must be demonstrated to the state licensing authority.

It the sales agent fails to comply with these legal requirements, the agent cannot renew the license after the first two years, and he or she is no longer allowed to practice in the real-estate sector. The infringement is illegal and constitutes a criminal offense under the licensing laws.

For you as a real-estate seller, it is important that you check that your sales agent has a valid license to be sure that the agent knows the duties and tasks within a real-estate transaction and that the agent is working under the supervision of a broker.

As soon as you have signed the listing agreement for your property with your real-estate specialist, the signing agent will assist you with your sale and represent you to other agents and buyers. The listing agreement—the contract for the exclusive marketing of your property—however, is between the responsible broker of the agent's real-estate office and you, not between you and the supervised agent. That means that the brokerage office has all rights to the listing and will receive the commission at closing, rather than the sales agent. The sales agent will get a share of the commission depending on the commission agreement between the brokerage office and the sales agent.

The brokerage office and its managing broker are responsible for the property handling of your real-estate transaction. This means, for you, that if the real-estate agent makes a mistake, the broker is liable for this error and not the supervised agent. How this error is subsequently settled between the agent and the broker is not your problem.

Which Tasks Will Your Listing Agent Perform for You?

Let us now look at the details of your listing agent who works for you in Florida. Because of the legal requirements, your real-estate specialist must be licensed in Florida, and the license must be valid and active. A real-estate agent from your home country cannot assist you with your transaction in Florida because that would be illegal and would be prosecuted as a criminal offense.

Your real-estate expert is your trusted person in the context of your property-sale transaction. The agent accompanies you through the entire sale process and explains the individual steps, how to complete them, which documents must be provided and submitted for the individual steps, and when each step has to be completed in order to fulfill the purchase-contract obligations successfully and on time.

Maybe you know the tasks of a real-estate agent in your home country; however, the tasks in Florida are different. A real-estate professional is not responsible solely for the marketing of your property but for the entire transaction. You will sign with your listing agent (broker) a listing agreement, in which your sales agent promises to market your property on the basis of statutory regulations in the best possible way and to present to you a potential buyer who is willing and financially capable of paying the desired listing price.

For you as the seller, this means that you work trustfully with your real-estate expert as a team and incorporate the agent's recommendations in your decision-making process. However, the necessary decisions are solely at your discretion, and your real-estate expert is not liable for your decisions.

Let us now look at the detailed tasks that you can expect from your real-estate specialist and that you should discuss with him or her so that there are no misunderstandings and problems in the transaction process later on.

During this conversation, which usually takes place on your property, you and your agent will walk through your property and its exterior area. In this visit the agent gets a first impression of the house and its best-selling features.

Before the visit the real-estate specialist will have already obtained the necessary documents regarding the ownership and financial situation of your property from the public records. As the term already implies, "public" means that any interested person can get this information from the Internet. These public records correspond to data that are reported in Germany in court records that you only can access with a special documented interest. In your home country, there may be other regulations for accessing such information. Data in the United States are much more detailed than in other countries and can be accessed legally at any time.

The visiting real-estate specialist will also have already selected a few comparable properties in your close area that are either offered on the market for sale or have been sold in the last six months. The agent will use these properties for an initial market valuation of your property.

With this information, and the inspection of your property with you, the agent gets a good picture of your home and existing questions, and missing details can be addressed and put together quickly and easily.

The supplementary information from you as the seller allows the real-estate specialist to refine and validate the prepared property evaluation for the possible sale price. The agent will discuss in detail the result of the value calculation with you and determine a listing price for your property sale based on this value calculation.

The calculated market value is also the basis for the determination of the commission percentage. The actual paid commission amount is later calculated based on the sale price at closing. If there is only one real-estate professional involved in the sale transaction, then this agent and the listing brokerage office are entitled to the entire commission amount. In the case of two involved real-estate professionals, the commission amount is evenly distributed between the two agents and their brokerage offices.

You as a seller can negotiate the percentage of the commission within the framework of your listing agreement with your listing brokerage office, but you have no influence on the distribution of the commission between the two brokerage offices. Any additional financial supplementary agreement, like a bonus when the property sells quickly or at a much better price than expected, must be communicated in order to avoid irregularities within the transaction later on.

Let us now turn to the tasks performed for you by your real-estate professional during the real-estate transaction.

As a first step, your real-estate agent will request all the necessary documents from you so that he or she knows the important details for the listing in the MLS—the multiple listing service, the listing database for successful marketing. Some of this information is directly and automatically transferred from the public records, and missing data have to be entered manually by the agent. All these details produce a clear picture of your property to potential purchasers and their real-estate specialists. The buyer can already decide on this basis if the property is interesting for him.

Furthermore, your listing agent will take pictures of your property from the inside and the outside to push the interest in your property on the Internet even more. In order to achieve the best results, your agent will give you some recommendations on how to create and improve the curb appeal of your home.

The most important recommendation is that your property is visually in perfect condition. That means the garden is in excellent shape, and there is no damage in and at the house. It is unnecessary to tell you that your home needs to be spotlessly clean everywhere.

Your real-estate agent will also coordinate with you when you open your property for the showings to buyers. In case of a showing, the buyer's real-estate consultant asks your agent for an appointment, so that buyer's agent can show your property to the customer.

Your presence is not desired at such a showing because it is hard for you, the seller, to keep your mouth shut and not gush in the highest tones about your home. For the purchaser, such enthusiasm can become daunting because the buyer usually already has an attitude toward your property that will be destroyed or at least influenced by your narrative. Our experience shows that such a change of feelings for a home is rarely positive for you, the seller. You may lose an interested and potential buyer.

To make such showings easier, your listing agent will ask you for a replacement key to your property and enter without your presence. This key is intended for the lockbox that is installed at one of your entrance doorknobs.

A few years ago, the lockbox was a small box with a number or letter combination. Today, there are tools called electronic lockboxes in place, which can be opened with a smartphone code. The smartphone transmits a unique identifier to the lockbox, and the lockbox releases the compartment with the key. At the same time, the lockbox registers the release of the key and sends the identification of the opening agent to the listing agent or the listing office. This message always documents who was at what time and for how long in your property for a showing. The showing agent is also responsible to ensure that the entrance door is properly locked when he or she leaves with the customer.

The real-estate expert enters the listing property with the purchaser and walks with the buyer through your home. After explaining the interior and exterior features of the property, the agent closes the home and puts the key back into the lockbox for the next visit of a real-estate professional with another customer.

Another popular way to market your property is the open house. At an open house, your real-estate expert publishes a date on the Internet when your property will be open to the public for viewings. On this day, your real-estate agent will ask you to leave your home for a few hours, and he will be at your home with a coworker and show your home to potential buyers who are passing by. These buyers have not yet decided if they want to purchase any home, but they have the opportunity to get an impression of a suitable property that they can afford. Such interested buyers are usually not accompanied by their own real-estate consultant, or they might not even have one.

When the first purchaser makes an offer, your real-estate agent will be there to help you. You will discuss together the offer of the purchaser, and the agent will explain to you the benefits and the pitfalls of the received purchasing contract.

There are some details regarding the government's financing specifics and funding programs that you should know. These details are frequently changing and may result in additional costs for you as the seller. This applies especially in connection with FHA or VA loans from government agencies.

When it comes to the legal explanation and interpretation of the contract paragraphs of the offer, you will need to contact your own real-estate lawyer for a consultation, because such activities are beyond the scope of expertise of a real-estate professional.

As real-estate professionals, we are allowed to fill the open spaces in the standard contract that are prepared by the Florida Bar Association, but we are not allowed to provide legal explanations and comments on passages of the contract. That would be legal advice, which may only be given by a licensed attorney.

However, due to our large business-contact database, we can provide you with a list of professionals for nearly every field—attorneys, title companies, tax consultants, finance specialists, and many more. This list represents only a selection of professionals and does not include a recommendation or assessment of the performance of the professionals.

As real-estate professionals, we are not allowed to conduct direct referrals. We may only present a selection to the customer, and kickbacks or gifts for the transfer of these business contacts are prohibited. Even a bouquet of flowers or a box of chocolates can be regarded as bribery. No trustworthy real-estate specialist wants to be exposed to that risk and will always try to avoid it.

With the signing of the listing contract, the following services are available to you, as well as the intensive marketing of your property on the Internet. An important step in the marketing process is the entry of your property into the above-mentioned MLS real-estate database.

The entry into this MLS database must be done within twenty-four hours after the signing of the listing contract. When your property is entered into that database, your property data will be distributed to over a thousand websites and web portals in the United States and internationally. Your listing will be translated into at least thirteen languages, such as Chinese, Japanese, Vietnamese, and of course German, French, and Spanish, to name only a few. Each user of these websites is a potential buyer for your home.

When all these activities are done, you can relax and leave everything else to your real-estate specialist. He or she will market the property, manage the transaction, and, of course, keep you informed during the whole process.

With the signing of the listing agreement, your real-estate professional becomes your personal representative in all important negotiation steps during the transaction. The agent will conduct all conversations with other real-estate experts and accept inquiries about your property. The agent will not disclose any confidential information that you give him or her, and that is particularly true when it comes to information about your lowest sale price.

This personal and confidential trust relationship remains exclusively reserved for you, the seller, unless your real-estate professional also takes care of the tasks of the buyer. In such a case, your real-estate expert will have to limit the confidentiality position to you, the seller, if you accept this change.

The agent has to explain and discuss this restriction with you, and this conversation must be documented in writing. Your agent will become, with this document, a transactions agent who works for two parties—buyer and seller—in a limited capacity.

That means, for you, that confidential information will remain confidential, but as of the date of signing the above-mentioned document, your listing agent mutates into an intermediary of information and facilitator of activities within the transaction. The confidential information of the buyer, if the agent should receive such, will not be given to you or vice versa.

You should carefully think about this arrangement and decide if you would like to accept it, or if you'd rather ask your listing specialist to recommend the buyer to a coworker to represent the buyer's interests in this sale transaction.

We think a recommendation to a different agent is the best way to go because it prevents problems from arising during the transaction process and prevents the parties from feeling incorrectly represented. Such a feeling or presumption is bad for the sale transaction and can lead to a loss of confidence. Such bad feelings often contain the risk of a complaint of misrepresentation to the Florida Real Estate Commission—or FREC, the regulatory board for the real-estate business—or a costly court action. This should be avoided at all costs because it does not help anyone.

How the described tasks of a real-estate professional work within your sale transaction will be explained in detail further down in the book, in the chapter "The Property-Sale Transaction in the United States—Florida as an Example."

How Much Do Real-Estate Services Cost?

As already mentioned, when you decide to work with a specific real-estate professional, you will have to sign an agreement with the agent's brokerage office, called the listing contract.

This listing agreement secures the exclusive right of your agent's brokerage office to list and sell your property. For this service, which will be explained in detail in the next chapter, the brokerage office of your agent gets a commission, and, according to the legal regulations in the United States and the State of Florida, you, the seller, are responsible for paying the commission.

The actual percentage for the commission is 6 to 7 percent of the listing or sale price. With this amount, the services of your real-estate specialist are paid with the sale transaction.

However, if you hire your expert for other tasks that do not directly correspond to the real-estate agent's obligations within the transaction, these are additional services. These services, which are not covered by the commission agreement, must be paid separately. For example, if your agent needs to get additional keys for the showings, then you are responsible for these costs, and you have to reimburse the agent.

If you are marketing your property on your own without the assistance of a real-estate specialist, then you will have to do all the activities within the sale process yourself, because any service has its price. You will get what you pay for.

Details on the commission payment can be found in the chapter about the closing and settlement of your real-estate transaction further down in this book.

REALTOR

What Does "Realtor" Mean?

In many publications, you will find the term "Realtor," and it's possible you do not know exactly what that means.

"Realtor" is a protected term and may only be used by real-estate professionals who are members of the National Association of Realtors (NAR), which has its headquarters in Chicago, Illinois.

This organization represents the interests of the real-estate professionals and real-estate owners nationally and internationally.

Besides this representation of real-estate professionals, the association also has established professional standards for the real-estate industry.

These professional standards are summarized in the association's code of ethics. This code defines the rules and regulations with which real-estate professionals conduct their business and cooperate with you, the customer, as well as the public and other real-estate professionals.

Every year, there are legal changes in the real-estate laws and related areas, and therefore, these regulations are adapted annually to the latest business practices and legal requirements.

Every real-estate professional who joins the National Association of Realtors is obligated to act according to these regulations and rules (the code of ethics) and use them as a basis for his or her professional conduct. In order to be able to renew the license every two years, the real-estate specialist is required to take training on this subject and to vow to comply with this code of ethics at the end of the course. In return, the agent can use the legally protected title "Realtor" with his or her name.

The NAR also supervises compliance with these professional standards as well as the proper use of the protected title "Realtor." In the event of an infringement, the property expert will be warned by the NAR, and sanctions may be imposed.

Membership in the National Association of Realtors is not compulsory, and therefore, there are professionals in the business who are not members. These agents are not allowed to call themselves Realtors. Whether these agents choose to familiarize themselves with and obey the code of ethics is questionable.

Therefore, it is always advised that you choose a Realtor over a non-Realtor because the moral obligations for the real-estate professional are more binding. Realtors are proud to be part of this association, which not only upholds the quality of the business but also protect the members against organizational and governmental attacks, and that is a benefit for all members.

What Do the Abbreviations on the Business Card of a Real-Estate Expert Mean?

As soon as a real-estate agent has successfully passed his or her state exam and has received the license from the state, the agent can legally work in the real-estate business.

The knowledge in the real-estate sector regards common business practices—simple purchases and sales or leases. All of these transactions are performed by the real-estate agent under the supervision of the managing real-estate broker of the real-estate office.

Real-estate professionals in the United States work as independent contractors. That means a real-estate agent is not employed at the broker's office and does not receive a monthly salary. The agent works at his or her own expense, and any income comes from the commission at the closing of a transaction. All transactions are performed under the supervision of a broker.

Based on the assistance to and the supervision of the performed services, the agent's broker is entitled to a part of the earned commission when the sale closes. The size of this share depends on each real-estate company and is negotiated between the supervising broker and the agent of the office.

In addition to the basic required studies, there are many other complementary training courses available for agents dealing with specific real-estate sectors. These additional trainings have been created in cooperation with the National Association of Realtors (NAR) and are open to any Realtor. Every Realtor can decide if and when he or she will invest the money and time into such complementary studies.

These additional trainings do not usually count toward the continuing education courses that are required for the renewal of the license. These courses are add-ons that document that the real-estate specialist is engaged in and committed to the profession and the business. The more training an agent successfully completes, the better his or her knowledge and ability to serve you in your sale transaction become.

Here are some examples of additional educational trainings for internationally/globally engaged real-estate professionals: CIPS, TRC, and RSPS. The complementary training ABR is not limited to international transactions, but it focuses on real-estate purchase interests nationally and internationally.

Further interesting and related trainings a seller should look for are GRI, SFR, and BPOR. These training courses are exclusively related to national real estate and construction, and they indicate extensive knowledge of a listing agent in these business areas. Within a sale transaction, this knowledge is very valuable for the seller.

The above-mentioned educational trainings are described in detail on the following pages. Understanding each term will give you insight into the professionalism of a real-estate specialist and the conduct of business.

What does "CIPS" mean?

The abbreviation "CIPS" stands for Certified International Property Specialist, and this education is provided by the National Association of Realtors (NAR) in Chicago.

This additional training deals with international real-estate transactions and the business-culture differences in other countries.

The Realtor with this education is trained in dealing with foreign-national real-estate owners. You certainly have realized that a real-estate transaction in your home country does not run the same way as it does in the United States. Your sales agent has to pay attention to these details and take care of them.

My own personal experience gives a good example of what such a Realtor can do. I got my education in real-estate financing in the largest German bank. Later, I combined these experiences and knowledge with more real-estate study in Florida. Today, my brokerage specializes in all kinds of international real-estate and business transactions. In my case, I can connect both sides—the United States and Europe—and represent the cultural and business differences and diversity of each. That is an ideal combination not only in real estate but also in business.

What does "TRC" mean?

The second additional training, TRC, stands for Transnational Referral Certification. This refers to cross-border cooperation with real-estate specialists in other countries, some of the usual business activities for a Realtor with such an education.

This complementary education focuses on the collaboration with a broker from your home country based on applicable real-estate laws in Florida and the United States.

If, for example, you have a broker in your home country, this broker can cooperate in a real-estate transaction, with your permission, with a real-estate broker in the United States. Such cooperation is free of charge for you as the customer.

The cooperation or referral agreement is signed between the two real-estate specialists—the broker in your home country and the broker in Florida.

The referral agreement regulates to what extent the American real-estate professional may pay a referral fee to the foreign broker and how much this fee may be.

Referral agreements between a broker and a private individual, and the payment of a fee to this private individual, is illegal and can lead to loss of license by the broker who violates this law.

Such a referral fee can be lucrative for the broker in your home country, and it means little or no effort will be required for him. The real-estate person in your home country simply establishes the contact with a local Florida broker, and the American real-estate broker takes over all the tasks in Florida. From that moment, you are only the customer of the Florida real-estate professional.

What does "RSPS" mean?

Another additional training is the RSPS—Resort and Second Home Property Specialist. Such a specialist is focused on vacation residences—homes and condominiums—in the real-estate market.

Such a real-estate agent focuses real-estate transactions on lifestyle properties, like those giving access to golf courses or yacht clubs. These specialists are well versed in these market areas and will help you in selling such real-estate property. They will find exactly the kind of buyers that appreciate your property the most.

Such lifestyle properties require special care because not every property is suitable for every purchaser. For example, if your property is located in a golf community, the buyer should also be a golf lover. Besides the annual golf club fees, a residency in a golf community is subject to additional obligations that the buyer should know about before closing on such a transaction.

RSPS

Resort & Second-Home Property Specialist

What does "ABR" mean?

The complementary training ABR stands for Accredited Buyer Representative, an important specialty for the purchase of a property.

For a seller, this education is only of secondary importance, because in the case of a sales transaction, the real-estate professional is representing the interests of the seller, not the interests of the buyer. However, this training can help to smooth and ease the sale transaction because such an agent is also familiar with the buyer's motivations and how to respond best during a real-estate transaction. This understanding is priceless for you as the seller.

While your real-estate professional has the task of finding a suitable buyer, the buyer's agent has the task of finding a suitable, affordable property for the purchaser.

The task of the buyer's agent is to search for suitable properties and present a list of these homes. From this list, the buyer picks the properties he wants to see. Furthermore, the agent assists the purchaser at all steps of the transaction, monitors these steps, and helps the purchaser to get the necessary documents for his side of the transaction. The buyer's professional will also give him a hand in finding a matching attorney or a title company if this is necessary.

The buyer's agent is also the representative of the purchaser in the transaction, while the listing agent is negotiating for the seller.

What does "GRI" mean?

This abbreviation "GRI" stands for Graduate Realtor Institutes and includes multistage, deepening studies of all real-estate areas.

These areas include not only market knowledge and professional skills but also education and training with technical tools and systems. Another area concerns the legal requirements of the profession and the measures by which the real-estate expert provides the best service for the customers without being in conflict with the legal framework.

A graduated Realtor can also perform leasing and real-estate-managing tasks in addition to buying and selling real-estate properties. Additionally, this agent is familiar with the basic tax conditions of a transaction, but the agent will not provide any tax-return filings for the customers or give any tax advice.

This is an important designation that gives you, the seller, the assurance that the real-estate professional knows all methods and procedures in the business and will minimize your risk within the real-estate transaction.

NATIONAL
ASSOCIATION *of*
REALTORS®
REALTOR
Official Designation

GRADUATE,
REALTOR®
INSTITUTE

What does "SFR" mean?

An SFR designee is a real-estate expert who is familiar with the special sector of short sales and REO—bank-owned properties.

In a short-sale transaction, the owner/seller is in a financially difficult situation and can no longer meet loan obligations. The sale of such a property often includes problems during the transaction and produces higher costs on the path to the closing. Therefore, a short sale takes more time before it can close, and the assistance of an attorney on the seller side may be advised to protect the seller's financial interest.

An REO is a property where the foreclosure process is already finished by the lender, and the lender has taken possession of the property. The lender can be a bank or a private lender.

Such properties are often in poorly maintained condition because the homes have often stood empty for a long time, with the lender only maintaining what is urgent and absolutely necessary. To manage such selling transactions, the real-estate professional has to pay a bit more attention than in common transactions.

If you are a seller in a financially distressed situation, such a specialist is a good partner for you to get the job done.

SFR

SHORT SALES &
FORECLOSURE
RESOURCE

What does "BPOR" mean?

The last additional education described in this book is the Broker Price Opinion Resource—BPOR—an expert in the calculation of market values for real-estate properties.

These specialists have a lot of experience in researching all kinds of necessary data for the most accurate market evaluations. They are often hired by banks and lenders to calculate the market values of real-estate properties in these lenders' portfolios.

Such a valuation is used to determine the actual market value of a property at a particular location and at a particular calculation date. Due to dynamic real-estate market movements, such an evaluation is only valid for three to a maximum of six months. After this time period, the valuation must be redone or at least adapted to the changed market conditions and criteria.

For a seller, such a real-estate expert is invaluable because he or she can explain the market dynamics and assist in the price negotiations with the buyer within your sale transaction.

I myself did thousands of such evaluations for banks and lenders during my career and have many years of experience in this field.

About these Designations

This book has given only a small insight into the relevant complementary education and training of a Florida real-estate professional. This education list is not complete, and training for other available real-estate sectors that are not relevant to the scope of this book have not been included.

When you talk to American real-estate specialists, ask each agent about his or her addition training. These successfully acquired trainings of the National Association of Realtors are recognized in the real-estate business and are regarded as seals of quality for your real-estate professional

How Do You Find a Matching Real-Estate Professional?

It is like in any other business sector. You talk to several service providers and interview them. The appearance of each real-estate professional will determine how competent and pleasant you think he or she is. Based on this meeting experience, you will certainly choose the best one for your transaction.

You can also ask a friend, but please keep in mind that your friend is not you. Just because, for example, your friend can work together with real-estate expert A, this does not mean that you will have a positive experience too. The interpersonal relationship between the agent and you must match; otherwise, you will not be satisfied.

Do not trust recommendation and rating lists; they often do not show reality. These lists are often built by complacency reviews or marketing tools. Using these tools, the real-estate specialist who benefits wants to get ahead of the pack.

We receive several requests every day for such recommendations. The requesters want us to give them positive assessments even if we have never worked together and therefore do not know whether they work properly or how good their knowledge and abilities are.

Marketing companies also promise that their services can raise real-estate agents to the top of the list on Google and Facebook. There is a common opinion that a customer selects an agent for a planned real-estate transaction based on who he speaks to first, and that is often the person on the top of the list. Such a real-estate professional, however, might not be the best for you if your service expectations do not correspond to the services offered by the provider.

The better way for you to find the right agent will be by using your gut feeling and the above-described additional educational qualifications. All real-estate professionals will happily show you their credentials because they have nothing to hide but much to gain—your transaction. It is like in every business: class is better than mass.

That means that although there are masses of real-estate professionals, only a small group has first-rate training and experience in the international real-estate business. Such real-estate experts can help you with your needs and make your sale transaction a success, but these agents rarely praise themselves with the above methods.

For questions in this context, we invite you to contact us using the e-mail address at the end of the book.

Below, you will find an Excel spreadsheet that demonstrates the business differences of real-estate professionals in Germany and the United States. If you are not from Germany, you will have to adapt this sheet to the information in your home country.

	United States	Germany
Who pays the agent?	Seller	Buyer, seller, or both partially
What tasks does the agent perform?	Search, show, and manage the transaction	Only search and show
Who has keys to the property?	Each agent has access to every property	The key is either with the seller or with the agent office or agent who manages the property
Who writes the contract?	Agent writes the contract based on standard real-estate contract of the local state	Special attorney writes the contract; agent is rarely involved in this action
Are professional regulations required?	Yes, state license	No
Is continuing education required?	Yes, otherwise the license will expire and cannot be renewed after two years	No mandatory continuing education
What commission is charged?	6 percent of the sale price, paid by the seller	6 percent plus VAT paid by seller, buyer, or both based on agreement
Is this field legally controlled?	Yes, state control by the Florida Real Estate Commission, with punishment power, affordable and without court proceeding	No state control

What Does "Fair Housing" Mean?

This is a fixed term and can be defined generally as the antidiscrimination law in the real-estate business.

The United States is and has always been a melting pot of nations, even if some governmental forces try to limit this. As you certainly know, the Americans had and still have some ugly episodes in their history regarding the integration of foreign peoples from other cultural backgrounds—such as African Americans, Native Americans, and religious groups—and the United States has learned from this history and is still learning until today.

The Fair Housing Act and the code of ethics of the Realtors state that no discrimination is allowed in the following areas of life: color, race, nationality, disability, religion, age, family status, sex, and sexual orientation.

This law applies in all areas of life, but it especially applies in all areas of the real-estate business. The violation of this law has legal consequences, no matter who the perpetrator is. This means that you, the seller, are bound by this law too, even if you are not a US citizen but a foreign national.

This law is the reason your real-estate specialist will give you valuable hints regarding which remarks to avoid and how to prevent problems in this area when working with a purchaser.

The following remarks, for example, will be extremely dangerous in your real-estate transaction:

"I only want to sell to Germans [or British or French]."

"Please, only buyers who do not have children or animals."

"Please, no handicapped buyers," or something similar.

The real-estate specialist will tell you in such a situation that you have to accept every buyer who is able and willing to pay your requested sale price for your property. A refusal of the buyer based on one of the above-mentioned reasons is illegal and can lead in the worst case to an expensive court procedure.

Not only are you bound to this regulation, but your listing agent and broker are too. That means if the real-estate expert tolerates and/or supports such behavior, the agent is as guilty as you are. For the real-estate professional, a complaint of violation of the Fair Housing Act can mean the loss of the license and the possibility of working in the real-estate business.

Your First Meeting with Your Real-Estate Professional

Have you already thought about your requirements and goals for your property-sale transaction? Have you made your own checklist with questions for your potential real-estate professional?

Very good!

You know the property, in which you have lived the past few years, inside and out. You know what problems exist and what little issues your home has. You know the physical characteristics of the property, such as the number of bedrooms, the number of bathrooms, and also the structural condition of the building.

You know what you have remodeled and modernized in your home. You also know how much you have paid for these remodeling activities, and you certainly want to get these costs back when selling the home—right?

If you have financed your home with a mortgage, then you certainly know the exact open balance of the loan. This open balance must be paid back when you sell your home, and you have to find out what the perfect timing is to pay off the loan.

You only need the best local real-estate specialist for your needs, someone who will, together with you, evaluate all the known facts and show you the best way to be successful in your project—your property sale in a foreign country.

Your next step now is to invite some local real-estate experts to your home and discuss with them your requirements and expectations for your property sale.

At the first interview, the agent will visit you at your property and ask you many questions that are essential for the most successful marketing of your home and for the determination of the highest possible selling price in your area and real-estate-market situation.

The real-estate professional will reconcile this information with your expressed wishes and expectations and will show you his or her professional views on your sale transaction. During this first interview, you should address and discuss all issues that are on your mind so that there arise no problems in the cooperation with your chosen real-estate specialist in the future.

It is certainly possible to cancel an existing listing agreement with your real-estate expert, but financial consequences can arise in this context. If, for example, costs have already been incurred since the signing of the listing contract up to its termination, then you, the seller, are responsible for these costs and must pay them to the listing office. Or if the listing office has already presented you a willing purchaser, but you have not yet signed the purchase contract for your property at the termination date of the listing contract, then there may be a commission due.

With your signature below the listing agreement, you also determine which kind of terms and conditions you will accept when selling your property. For example, you can specify that you only accept cash buyers because such a transaction is not slowed down and complicated by the loan-approval process of the buyer.

You have to be careful when accepting FHA loans because you as the seller have to expect higher closing costs. FHA loans are special mortgages that are sponsored by the US government and that are available to buyers with low equity bases and low credit scores.

Furthermore, it is important to decide which items of the interior equipment will remain in the property and which you will take with you. A kitchen, for example, is considered to be firmly connected to the home and usually stays in the property. It is commonly the same with appliances, like the stove, refrigerator, hot-water heater, and air-conditioning unit.

Electric appliances, such as dishwashers, washing machines, and dryers, are not standard equipment for a property and are often taken by the seller when moving out.

All these details must be communicated to the sales agent so that this is entered and published correctly in the MLS—multiple listing service. On the basis of these MLS facts, the future purchaser will make the purchase offer, and in this offer, all items that are sold together with the property are listed separately. That protects you from misunderstandings later.

The listing agreement also determines whether you are a non-US citizen under FIRPTA (a tax act for foreign-national sellers of real estate in the United States).

There are also regulations in the listing contract regarding when you will allow showing and where the lockbox can be installed so that potential buyers can visit your home together with their agents.

Additionally, the contract defines the marketing methods that will be used, and these will be discussed with you if you have any restrictions for showings. However, when making restrictions of any kind, you should realize that you could torpedo your chance for a quick sale at the best price.

It makes little sense to expect a quick, high-price sale when asking your agent to do a pocket listing or drawer listing, as is common in some countries. With such a restricted listing, your sales agent cannot market your listing on public portals, but only e-mail his or her own customer database. Even if this database contains ten thousand or more customer contacts, it can mean that you will not receive an offer at your expected sale price.

On the other hand, when the listing agent markets the home publicly without any restrictions, this listing will appear on more than one thousand national and worldwide Internet sites and portals. Such a distribution gives you access to billions of users as soon as the listing is in the MLS database. Therefore, it is not recommended that you restrict the marketing efforts of your professional. Your property will be one of many, but it will also be seen by tons of interested buyers.

The following statistics give you a small insight into what the real-estate market looked like in January 2017 in Fort Lauderdale, Florida.

Of 5,486 active, listed single-family homes, 982 properties were sold, with an average sale price of $381,478. This average sale price is 5.6 percent higher than in January 2016.

Of 8,951 active, listed condominiums (condos), 1,088 condos were sold, with an average sale price of $197,877. This average sale price is 4.5 percent higher than in January 2016.

As you certainly know, every statistic is just a snapshot of the local real-estate market. There are many criteria that influence these statistics, and the property values are in constant motion. For example, the employment market, the available real-estate properties, and the loan conditions are only a few factors that have an impact on such statistics.

Ask your local real-estate expert about the latest real-estate market numbers to get an approximate idea of how long you will be staying in your home and how fast you'll need to find a new place to stay. When you price your home right, your moving date will be very close.

Staying in your home beyond the closing date is not recommended because there are often disputes between the former and new property owners regarding the rent and maintenance obligations for the property. Such disputes can end quickly before a judge in a courtroom.

This is a small guideline for the first interview with your real-estate specialist. We suggest that you create a checklist with your own questions, goals, and expectations.

How Can You Prepare Your Home for the Sale?

If you own a property in your home country or have already sold a property, you probably think that everything will go exactly the same way as at home. That is not the case. In the United States, it is much different from what you may know from your home country, and the real-estate laws of your home country cannot be transferred, one to one, to the United States or Florida. Something that is allowed in your home country and is considered common can be prohibited in a foreign country, which brings disadvantages.

Even when you cross the borders to a neighboring country in Europe, your real-estate knowledge is no longer valid. There are more or less large differences between Great Britain, France, and Germany, and the differences between the United States and Europe are even bigger in comparison to those across Europe.

Let us now shift our focus back to the real-estate sale in Florida. How you should make your decision as to whether to sell and why you are selling was covered in the chapters above.

What services and activities a real-estate professional in Florida provides for you have also been explained, and the execution of these services will be described in the section of this book about the real-estate transaction.

The next point on our list regards your own tasks during the sale transaction. It is not enough that you hire your real-estate expert to market your property. Your home must be at least market average in comparison to other homes to attract many interested buyers who will pay your price.

If your property corresponds to the average of your neighbor properties, you will only receive the average selling price for that community. You surely want a better price—don't you? Every dollar you make above the average sale price will be a dollar more for your future dreams and goals, whatever those may be.

What do we mean by that? It's very simple—to stand out from the mass of the real-estate properties on the market, you can improve with many small things your curb appeal (attractiveness of your property).

Measures to increase curb appeal are not necessarily expensive and can often be done quickly, with a bit of work and sweat. However, all visual repairs should be done before your real-estate professional comes for the photo shoot of your home.

These property pictures are essential for successful online marketing, and appealing real-estate photos attract many more purchasers than ugly ones. The more buyers are interested, the more quickly the first buyer will make an offer. The faster you sell your home, the faster you will get your money and be allowed to concentrate on your new goals.

Here are some suggestions for how you can raise the curb appeal of your property. The following recommendations are based on our experiences as real-estate brokers, having completed many transactions.

Thorough housecleaning for the sale

Let us start with the simplest ways to increase the value of your property: cleaning every corner of the rooms and house. By this we mean more than removing spider webs, which are often found in Florida and which speak of a dry home.

We also do not only mean cleaning and scrubbing the floors, bathrooms, and kitchen but also removing the lime on fittings and the rust spots on countertops, storage spaces, and cabinets.

In the bathroom, the drain pipes underneath the sink and in the bathtub are to be freed from clogging and soap residue so that the water drains without accumulation.

The greasy film from cooking and frying must be removed from the cooking top and the backsplash area. The refrigerator and the ice compartment must be defrosted and cleaned. By removing the grease, you reduce cooking odors, and the cooling performance of the refrigerator improves with the removal of ice residue.

If you want to sell your washing machine and dryer with the house, you should clean the washer of detergent residues on both the inside and outside. The lint filter in the dryer must also be without any fluff so that both appliances look well maintained.

When it comes to the air-conditioning system, you should replace the air filter and clean the covers of the air inlets and outlets. Please check the ventilation shafts in the property, and hire a professional company for the cleaning of the shafts if necessary.

The need for cleaning the windows and doors is self-evident; you certainly know that a home looks much brighter and nicer when it is sun drenched.

With these tips, you can give your home a fresh and attractive look, and air-freshener boxes throughout the property will do the rest. Potential buyers will love your home when they do not smell your personal scent and do not discover the limestone marks of the past few months.

These tricks not only improve the appearance of your property but also help with the buyer's upcoming home inspection, which is described in one of the following chapters.

Little patching activities before the sale

In the previous section, we looked at measures for the sale that you can take without any additional expenses. However, there are also things that cannot be resolved with only sweat, water, and soap.

If, for example, your faucets are old and ugly, but your bathroom is relatively modern looking, then it makes no sense to renovate the entire bathroom to add value. In such a case, it is recommended that you replace the fittings with new ones, which has the same effect and is less expensive.

It is also a good idea to go through all rooms and make small, inexpensive cosmetic updates. For example, fill little dowel holes in the walls with some plaster. In Florida, there is rarely wallpaper in homes, so it is easy to patch these holes and then make the spots invisible with a little matching paint color. You can mix the matching color based on a little flake of the existing color.

In case your children tried to be Picasso and have decorated your bedroom walls with paintings, you will not be able to avoid a complete painting of the room in a modern, attractive color.

Nothing is more upsetting to a potential buyer than visible neglect of your home. A buyer will not tell you that directly, but the offer that the buyer may write will speak to you in a loud and clear voice.

For more suggestions, you can contact us by e-mail because we are interested in helping you sell your property at the highest possible price.

Yard makeover before the sale

So far we have concentrated our efforts on the interior of the home, but now we will look at the garden with its vegetation and—if existing—the pool, the boat dock, and the patio.

If you have a pool in the yard, it should be filled with clean blue water. It is certainly unnecessary to mention that the pump and all cleaning devices of the pool should be in excellent condition.

Of course, the pool deck should be cleaned with a high-pressure washer and have no ugly, dirty spots. The outdoor furniture on the patio should have no stained or patched cushions and covers.

Peeled paint on the exterior walls or on the yard fence is not acceptable and must be redone before the first potential purchaser comes for a showing.

As soon as the property is on the market, the lawn must be mown short and the plant beds and borders kept free from weeds. Another no-go in the yard are dried palm leaves that either dangle down or are scattered around on the lawn.

The irrigation system of the yard must be functional and should ensure that your yard looks like an inviting green oasis to every potential purchaser.

The mailbox and the house number on the exterior wall must be in good condition so that it is easy for a buyer to find your property.

Getting the property documents together

After inspecting the interior and exterior appearance of your property, we will take the real-estate documents and get them together.

You certainly know best how real-estate documents are handled in your home country. In Germany, the property documents are recorded and reported in the land registry. This land registry is a registry at the local district court, and all the information that is documented there is believed valid and credible.

Access to this land registry is limited, and only a person that can prove an important reason can investigate these documents. In case of a legitimate interest, the requesting person can ask for an abstract and has to pay a fee for that abstract.

In the United States, this information is handled differently. All documents in connection with a real-estate property are public records and can be examined at any time and by anybody. It is not required that anyone show a reason for the request, and there are no costs involved.

As a real-estate professional, I can always look at all public records and print a copy of the document I need. For each property, there are documents about the lot, sales contracts, tax records, and much more.

You as a property owner should be able to produce these original documents to your real-estate expert upon request for inspection.

Among other things, the important papers include the annual property tax bill and the documentation that you have paid these taxes on time.

In case the tax was not paid, the tax amount due will be deducted from the sale proceeds at closing and transferred to the local tax authority.

These documents also include papers that have been registered with the court in connection with any divorces or inheritances. These papers are necessary to prove your ownership of the real-estate property beyond a reasonable doubt.

If you own a home, you should also have a survey of your property. In Germany, these papers are called Katasterpapiere, and they document the exact size and location of the property boundaries. In the United States, only the owner has this document, and it is done especially for the owner by a surveying company that gets paid for this service.

If you have never had a survey or do not have these papers anymore, this does not matter to you. As a seller, you do not have to provide this document, and the potential buyer has to get his own survey at his own costs. You are not obligated to provide this document, but sometimes the buyer will try to force you to pay for it.

Which repairs did you do during your ownership— and when?

We have already described some improvements you could make to your property. These recommendations are small corrections to the appearance of your property, with the goal to increase sales revenue.

Let us now talk about repairs, modernizations, and renewals that you made during your period of ownership of your property.

Such alterations include roof replacement, window and door exchange, as well as the modernization of the interior power lines and plumbing pipes. These modernization or alterations are activities that are subject to the applicable Florida building codes. For these improvements, you will need the appropriate permits from your municipality.

For these building projects, you have to apply for a permit at the building department of your city before you start. The building department has to grant the permit before your constructor executes the remodeling tasks. During the improvement process, the responsible building inspector will inspect the work and approve it. Upon the work's completion, the inspector makes the final inspection and issues an occupation certificate. With this completion document, your construction project is successfully finished and will be archived in the public records.

This construction documentation is extremely important for the sale because if these documents are missing, this may be an indication that the owner altered the home illegally. The owner is liable for this offense and will receive a fine. The missing documents also create a cloud on the deed (an error in the property documents), and this cloud must be resolved before the sale transaction can be closed. Details on this topic can be found in the chapter on the title investigation, a process that you may have in your home country too.

This permit process is not limited to interior home alterations, but also applies to home extensions and other outdoor changes, such as the building of a pool or a fence.

If there are still outstanding invoices in connection with your construction project, these invoices will lead to a lien on the property. These liens are comparable to a lender's or tax lien and have to be paid off at the closing table of your sale transaction.

How old are the appliances on your property, and do you have warranty contracts?

Let us now talk about the last topic that you should not neglect, because at least at the buyer's home inspection, you will be asked these questions.

Each electrical appliance in your home has a standard lifetime. This lifetime is used to evaluate at the home inspection how long the appliances will still be functional and when an exchange can be expected.

This information may affect the purchase price of the property. Should the equipment of the home be at the end of its life expectancy, then the buyer can take that as a reason for price negotiations. If your appliances are at the end of the standard lifetime, the purchaser has to expect to replace them within a short period of time, and that will increase his expenses for the purchase and possibly exceed his financial resources.

Perhaps you own a home warranty contract. Such a contract covers all repair and replacement costs for electrical appliances in the home during the contract period. Such a contract is usually transferrable to the new owner for the rest of the contract period. Consequently, the buyer has to decide if he or she wants to continue the warranty contract or not.

You should not confuse this warranty contract with homeowner's insurance. Homeowner's insurance covers damages caused by storms, water, or fire, and this insurance is not transferable.

Besides homeowner's insurance, many property owners in Florida also need flood insurance because of the low level of the lots, the storm surges, and the coastal flooding. Whether such insurance is necessary for your home can be checked on the state flood maps. Your insurance company can tell you if this insurance is transferable.

Why Are the above Details Important for Your Sale?

We're sure you took the above suggestions to heart: to push the curb appeal of your home because the attractive first impression is the best path into the heart of your potential buyer. The nicer the impression is, the more likely it is that the buyer will make a high-price offer.

A take-it-or-leave-it mind-set is definitely not the correct one for a successful real-estate sale in Florida. With your property, you are only one participant in a gigantic real-estate pool, where only the fittest earn the largest reward—a high sale price.

You must decide for yourself whether you consider the above tips to be valuable and important. As nearly always in life, your motivation for the property sale is as important as the price goal for the sale.

If you sell your current home because you want to buy a bigger one or live at a more exclusive location, then it should be in your interests to get the highest possible sale price for your home. You will only achieve that goal if your home has an excellent curb appeal and is in better-than-average condition. For your goal, your home must be in the upper tier of the available comparable properties in your neighborhood.

With a high sale price, you will have more liquidity for your new dream home, and the necessary funding share will be lower. This will result in not only a lower monthly loan payment but also in a faster payoff of the mortgage.

If your motivation is to move into a smaller home, then perhaps the highest sale price comes second to the fastest and easiest handling of the sale transaction. In this case, it will be sufficient that your property does not require major renovation at the closing and that all the appliances in the home are functional and in working condition.

In case you sell in a financially distressing situation—because you can no longer pay your monthly loan payments, for example—then the thoughts about updates and modernization are superfluous. You simply do not have the money to pay for them; otherwise, you certainly would not sell your home.

When you have inherited the property and want to sell it, then you should consult with an attorney and a tax consultant to analyze your existing situation. Only when you have the advice of both can you make the best decision on how much money and time you want to invest in the above-mentioned recommendations. Otherwise you will not get back the invested money at the closing table.

If you are confused now or have further questions, we will be happy to assist you in making the right decision. Please send your questions to the e-mail address at the end of the book.

Now Your Real-Estate Professional Takes Over

As a seller, if you have executed some of the above-mentioned recommendations, you are now very well prepared for the next steps and can sit back and wait for the buyers. Your real-estate professional will take over for the next activities.

Your task is now to wait patiently for the first buyer with an offer and be ready for any questions that your listing agent may have for you.

According to the agreed listing contract, your real-estate expert will take all necessary steps for a successful sales transaction.

As a first step, your real-estate broker will send you a copy of the listing contract and work out with you the preparations for a photo shoot of your home.

You should clean up your home and remove all personal items that can deter a purchaser. The same applies to items that you do not want to sell with the property; otherwise, your buyer might fall in love with that item and want your home only with that specific item in it. We do not speak of furniture but of unique lamps or chandeliers.

Please do not forget to take your jewelry and medication out of the property or at least lock these items in a secure box or cabinet.

When the above tasks are done, then the listing agent will take professional photos of your property and will upload them to the MLS—multiple listing service. These photos, as well as all important data regarding your property, are distributed nationally and worldwide to affiliated Internet sites and portals.

The lockbox with the replacement key to your property is installed at one of your entrance doors, and the available showing times are entered into the MLS. Now each buyer's agent can electronically request a showing for the potential purchaser.

You will tell your agent what kind of financial funding you will accept and how much earnest money (definition to follow in the chapter about the title company) you want to request from your buyer. You will also decide if you are willing to make repairs and make sure you have already selected a title company for the transaction process.

After the photo shoot, your agent will provide you with marketing flyers, which you can provide to your friends, neighbors, and other acquaintances. For visiting potential buyers, such a flyer is also a good advertising tool because it serves as a reminder for your buyer.

Another marketing tool that is common in Florida is a yard sign of your listing office and real-estate expert in the front yard of your home. It offers the possibility for any passing drivers or neighbors to contact your agent for more details about your home.

However, potential buyers should not use you as an information resource; you may reveal discouraging information about your home that will weaken your negotiating position in the transaction. In addition, such a conversation can quickly lead to emotional discussions about your home that can affect your sale opportunities. You have hired your real-estate expert precisely for this communication task and for response to inquiries.

Your real-estate specialist will do all the necessary negotiations and paperwork for you and reduce your risk of making expensive mistakes. Sellers going the FSBO ("for sale by owner") route have to complete all these tasks and discussions themselves. Such sellers take the full risks of their actions and errors upon themselves.

We've described all the important details for the sale transaction, and now it is time to complete such a successful sale transaction on paper. In this way, you will gain insight into what you have to expect and how you can help within the individual steps of the transaction to finish the deal quickly and successfully for yourself.

Here we go!

THE PROPERTY-SALE TRANSACTION IN THE UNITED STATES—FLORIDA AS AN EXAMPLE

After having explained the real-estate business in the United States and Florida, we can move on to the next step: the successful marketing of your property and its profitable sale.

You are certainly already curious about how you can sell your property at the highest possible price. It is imperative that you inform yourself in advance about the most important decisive aspects of your project, your property sale in a foreign country, and that you first think on the necessary measures to achieve that goal. You now have a clear idea of what to expect from a real-estate professional and how the real-estate agent will assist you on your path to your goal.

Your new knowledge, acquired in the first chapters, will make it much easier for you to find the right property specialist. You know what you should ask your expert, and you will notice very quickly if the real-estate professional knows the business and what he or she is talking about. Your agent should not ignore your questions and concerns.

Now it is much easier to ask the most difficult questions and discuss them intensively with your expert. You have a clear vision of what sale revenue you expect and how you want to achieve that result.

Such preparation is much more pleasant and satisfying for you than relying on neighborhood and friends' gossip. This gossip will not support your needs and will depend often on the personal feelings of your neighbors or your friends.

Never forget that what has worked for your friends or neighbors might not work for you and your project, property sale in a foreign country, too. Each property is unique and must be marketed accordingly. You and your real-estate specialist will be a well-established team, and no stone in the path to closing will stop you.

Your real-estate specialist will explain to you the individual steps of the sale-transaction process in the United States, which is completely different from that of many other countries in the world. The real-estate specialist has to work on a much more comprehensive task list than one would, for example, in Germany, and he or she will be at your side at each step on the way. Your real-estate expert is the focal point of your sale transaction and will complete the transaction successfully—with you and with the best possible outcome for you.

Your real-estate agent will present the complex sale process easily and comprehensively for you, so you can make your necessary decisions quickly and without any hassles to sell the property. You will soon be on the road to new goals, with the sale proceeds in your pocket. Only if you are a happy seller will your real-estate broker be happy too—because the agent only gets a commission when the buyer has paid and the property has a new owner.

Let us kick off your project, *property sale in a foreign country.*

Basics for the Seller

Once you have signed the listing agreement with your real-estate specialist, you only live for a time in your home or condominium. With the assistance of your agent's marketing, your home will be presented to billions of potential buyers. If a buyer is interested, the buyer will ask for a showing. This is especially the case when the property is intended to be the primary residence for the purchaser.

If the property is bought as an investment, then a personal visit is not always necessary, but a house inspection should be expected in all cases. In the United States, the principle is "buyer beware"—which means a buyer should be smart and check the property before making an offer.

The real-estate seller must not conceal any defects, but he need not disclose every little detail. The rule is that the seller has to provide all information that affects the material value of the property. Such information is, for example, that the roof may start to leak because it is at the end of its lifetime. The home inspector has to give out that information.

The buyer has to think about what is important to him and find these details out for himself by means of smart questions and a home inspection, even if such a home inspection is not usual in the buyer's home country. The buyer should never rely on the information of the seller, but only on the facts of a competent professional.

Seller Preparation for Property Showings to Purchasers

If your listing agent has not yet prepared you for the first showing to a potential purchaser, then it is time to do so now. You cannot treat a buyer's showing like a visit from friends or family.

A visit from family or friends at your birthday or for a little small talk is not comparable to a visit from the critical eyes of a buyer at a showing.

When your potential purchaser comes for a showing, he or she must be wowed by your kitchen, bathrooms, and bedrooms. Dust and dust bunnies are not acceptable. The bedrooms and closets should be tidy, clean, and orderly. Collared blouses and T-shirts in the closet and dirty laundry on the floor will give the buyer a bad impression of you. This makes it easy for the purchaser to transfer this impression to other areas of your home, such as maintenance efforts.

Your family and friends know you by heart. If a pillow is not placed properly on the couch during a visit, they may not care—but a purchaser does care.

The same applies to personal things, such as family photos. For family members and friends, such pictures are an OK and attractive accessory for your home, but for a buyer, such details can be disruptive. When the purchaser comes into your home, he wants to feel like the new owner of your home. This rarely works when your family smiles at the buyer from your pictures on the wall.

Besides the family photos, you should also put away or lock up your jewelry, other valuables, and medications. We do not want to tell you that buyers are thieves and will steal, but you certainly understand that a real-estate specialist cannot keep an eye on every individual buyer when more than one comes for a showing. Maybe you know the saying "Opportunity makes thieves"; that should not happen to you.

After these obvious tidying-up activities, clearing up is also a good idea. We know it is often difficult to get rid of things that you no longer use. After all, you never know if you may need one thing or the other in the future. However, if you want to sell your property at your desired price, then you must act and clear up your home.

Clearing up has to include your garage and laundry room with the washing machine and dryer. These spaces often do not get the attention they need, and the buyer will notice your carelessness.

For the buyer, an orderly, maintained washer and dryer are important because they often remain in the home, and no buyer wants to buy neglected appliances. The same applies to the hot-water heater and the air handler of the air-conditioning system, which are often located in the garage or the laundry room.

The hot-water heater should not show any rust and should have an energy-proof label. The washer and dryer should be clean too, without any rust and without lint in the lint filter. The exhaust hose must be cleaned as much as possible or replaced with a new one. It is unnecessary to say that these areas should look well organized.

Besides disorder, clutter is a big problem in a property. Clutter means a lot of stuff and mess, and that scares buyers away. This junk is often collected in all rooms, in the laundry room, and in the garage. Maybe it is hard for you to throw that stuff away because it cost you a lot of money in the past.

Bedroom

For a showing, this clutter is unacceptable. This stuff has to go because it makes the rooms and garages look smaller, giving the buyer the impression that it's a smaller property, when in reality, it's exactly the size he is looking for.

There are several solutions to this matter. The first one is a garage sale, where you sell all your stuff that is too good to be thrown away. Maybe you know the words "Someone's trash is another one's treasure"—your garbage may be a trophy for somebody else.

In such a garage sale, you can earn a little money for your clutter. However, you cannot expect to get the price you paid for it, even when the item is unused. Such a sale is still better than putting the stuff at the roadside for the garbage trucks.

Another option is to put your stuff into a storage unit in one of many private warehouses. Such a storage unit is absolutely necessary before the first showing so that the superfluous clutter is stored safely. Unnecessary and bulky furniture, decorations, or boxes reduce the size of every room and always look very messy.

A purchaser is always interested in getting the largest possible property for the smallest possible price. To achieve this, everything has to be removed, and we really mean everything that diminishes the space. The remaining pieces of furniture should be placed so that the rooms look big and inviting to every interested purchaser.

Another potential flaw in a property is its smell. If, for example, you are a smoker and have smoked inside the property, it is essential to eliminate this smell. Or if you have animals, it is absolutely necessary to cover this animal smell and remove the animals completely, at least during a showing to a potential purchaser. Not every buyer likes animals and certainly not the smell of them.

As was already mentioned above, smell and cleanliness are a seller's first priorities when presenting your home. This also applies to the bathrooms and the kitchen.

In the bathrooms, water and lime stains on the sink and bathtub as well as on the fittings are not acceptable. These stains show negligence in the care of the bathrooms. Also, the tiles and grout between the tiles should be scrubbed vigorously with vinegar cleaner and a brush to remove any stains.

You should also consider whether it might make sense to replace old-fashioned fittings with more modern ones. Such an update can be achieved with little money but can have a big impact. The purchaser will get the impression that the bathroom or the kitchen has been recently remodeled.

Small defects and damages to walls or doors can be quickly fixed with the appropriate means from do-it-yourself stores. These efforts do not cost much, but they can produce a big, effective impression.

If the damages are bigger, or if the paint in one of the rooms is distracting for the purchaser, then you should quickly buy a bucket of paint and a painter roll and change the color. The salesperson in the do-it-yourself store can tell you which color and in what consistency is the right one. These salespeople are often valuable resources for all your remodeling needs and will give you the best tips for your renovation project.

Before you start your renovation project, it is recommended that you make a cost-benefit analysis. The expenses that you pay to make your home more attractive and appealing to the purchaser should be in the correct proportion to the possible increase of the sale price. It does not make sense to spend thousands of dollars on remodeling if that renovation only means a few dollars in return at the closing table. Such unnecessary renovations are, for example, high-end golden fittings and faucets in a middle-income community.

After the interior makeover of your home to impress the buyer is complete, we now turn to the outdoor features. This part of your home is almost more important than the interior of your home. When a purchaser approaches your home, the exterior image is the first impression the buyer gets.

Exterior view

If the exterior already demonstrates neglect of the home, then the interior features of the property can rarely compensate for that. The exterior has already created an opinion in the head of the buyer, and that opinion will affect all further impressions and will lead to a decision against your home.

The first step to creating well-maintained outdoor features is to ensure that the lawn always looks freshly mown and that the shrubs and hedges are always cut. If the lawn grows too tall and the shrubs too wild, it not only looks ugly but can also lead to penalties from the municipality. Every city has regulations on garden maintenance because the vegetation in Florida grows fast and wild and then offers shelter to unwanted animals.

Another important point regarding the maintenance of outdoor features is the treatment of the pool and pool deck. A pool always includes a cleaning system and a circulation pump that ensure that the water does not turn green and become a mosquito breeding ground. Mosquitoes are native inhabitants of Florida, and they are under control today as long as standing waters are treated and maintained; otherwise, the numbers would explode and endanger the residents.

You also must ensure that the pool is always filled with water so that it will not get damaged. The water in the pool is necessary so that the pool builds up enough pressure against the surrounding soil. If the pool doesn't contain enough water, the surrounding soil can push out the pool and damage the pool and the pool deck.

For luxurious properties, one important feature is the private boat dock in the backyard. As the owner of such a property, you are responsible for the maintenance of the dock as well as the seawall, which secures the shoreline. When selling such a luxury property, you should pay attention to the structural details of the feature; otherwise, the purchaser will make a reduced offer because you have neglected your obligations.

Additionally, you should pay attention to possible grandfathered rights in connection with the boat dock. Not all docks comply with the applicable city codes, and in case of damage or neglect, the city may require you or the future owner to adapt the dock to the existing building codes. Your potential buyer will not accept such a flaw without a purchase-price reduction. Therefore, it is recommended that you investigate the facts.

Your patio or porch should also be in excellent condition and invite your potential buyer to rest. A strong power washer can quickly remove dirt in that area. Meanwhile, new cushions on the yard furniture are only a small investment, but they create a big effect.

If you have an outdoor mosquito-screening construction around your pool and patio area, then it is a good idea to make sure that this construction has no damage. Every detail indicates to the buyer whether you pay attention to the maintenance of this valuable property feature.

Please also critically check the exterior walls of your home, and repair color damage and color changes. For example, color changes can occur when you irrigate your lawn with well water from your lot. Often, the pump system produces rust particles that settle on the outer coat of the wall and lead to ugly brown spots. Such spots can be removed quickly and easily with a detergent from the hardware store, and a new paint coat is often not necessary.

After our step-by-step explanation, please never forget this: any action you perform in connection with the real-estate sale transaction has only one purpose, to make your home look like the cream of the real-estate market. The buyer must immediately imagine himself as the new owner when entering your home and backyard. Your real-estate tastes and feelings are no longer relevant at this time.

To find out how successful you are in presenting your home to potential buyers, you should ask your listing broker to request feedback from each and every showing. With this feedback, you will find out if you have met the taste of the buyers in the market. You also will find out where you should polish your home a little bit more to get the best possible impression and generate the highest possible sale price.

You have now prepared everything, and you are ready for the first showing. It will certainly not remain the only one. If your home is perfect looking and stands out in the crowd, then potential purchasers will come and visit like crazy. Stay confident and positive—the right buyer will come sooner or later.

The First Offer—What Now?

The showings of your home have started well, and many prospective buyers have visited your property in recent days, but so far, no offer has come. You may feel somewhat disappointed and frustrated with the situation. Perhaps you did not agree with the feedback of the interested purchasers. Do not worry!

Please do not get discouraged. It takes a little time until enough potential buyers have visited your property, either on the Internet or in reality. You and your property are in direct competition with many other properties on the market. Also, each prospective purchaser has his own very personal expectation regarding what is most appealing to him in a property. That can be the floor plan, the style, the backyard, the age, or the Florida charm, et cetera. All of these buyers' wishes cannot affect you unless you want to change your whole property for each particular buyer. You surely do not want that.

You should listen to the feedback obtained from potential buyers after the showings without any emotion and should critically compare the feedback with reality. Sometimes feedback is extremely helpful because you've put on your sunglasses and overlooked little flaws in your home. For you, everything is beautiful and appealing, but that may not be the case for the potential new owner. Try to see the feedback objectively, as suggestions for improvement potential in the presentation of your home.

Feedback that is obviously wrong or exaggerated, such as that the pattern of the floor tiles is ugly, you can ignore. This purchaser is not the one for your property, and his feedback is not meant honestly, but as an auxiliary claim. Your real-estate broker will confirm that based on his business experience.

An important piece of feedback that you should pay attention to if you've spent maybe three or four weeks on the real-estate market without a purchase offer is the desired listing or selling price. When you signed the listing agreement with your broker, he certainly gave you a listing-price recommendation based on the real-estate market conditions at that time. This listing price needs to be matched with the actual and changing market conditions every month and, if necessary, adjusted. For this adjustment of the listing price, the listing broker has to consider the prices of other actual listed and recently sold properties and compare the results with your listing price.

The properties currently listed on the market show your direct competitors with regards to the buyers, while recently closed transactions indicate your chances of selling your property for your desired sale price.

If your listing price is below that of recently closed transactions, then your listing price is not the problem. In such a case, the problem is in the condition or the presentation of the property. Potential buyers do not see themselves as the future owners of your home, and the reason could be, for example, that the kitchen has a somewhat outdated design or that the air-conditioning system is too old and uses too much electricity. An important indication of what is wrong with your home could have been given in the feedback from buyers who've had a showing of your home.

With a listing price above that of recently closed transactions, your listing price may be too high. Your property, its conditions, and its equipment might perhaps be below the market average, so buyers might consider your listing price too high in comparison to the presentation of your home. In such a case, it is urgently needed that you get a recommendation in regards to the listing price from your real-estate professional. He is your best partner in this field. Your agent has the most extensive market knowledge and can advise you on the adjustment of the listing price.

If you do not do this evaluation of the market every month, you might find yourself sitting on your property while other real-estate owners who listed later but are more closely oriented to market changes already have offers for their properties.

You should not stick too rigidly to your desired sale price; stay flexible, and orient yourself to the market changes that your broker tells you of. The listing agent always has your goal in mind—the highest possible price for your home—because the higher the sale price, the higher the commission amount, and that is his income. When the agent advises you incorrectly, then he will earn less or nothing at all. Your expert will only receive his commission when you receive the sale price at the end.

If you discuss the above information with your broker, you will quickly know what to do and certainly make the correct decision in regard to further marketing efforts for your property. Each decision brings you closer to your goal—the sale of your property at the highest possible price.

Soon your real-estate professional will come with exciting news—a purchase offer for your home—and that is the next big step on the path to your goal.

An interested potential purchaser will make you this offer. The most important point in this offer is the purchase price that the buyer is willing to pay for your home. Besides the purchase price, the buyer will tell you how much earnest money—how big a deposit on the purchase price—he will pay, how he wants to pay the rest of the sale price, and what the desired closing date is.

If the purchase offer is interesting to you, it will be easy for you to accept the offer and sign it. With your signature, the buyer's offer will become a legally binding contract. Meeting with a real-estate lawyer for the preparation of the contract and certification of the deal, as occurs in Germany and other countries, is not necessary.

To get a better understanding of such a purchase contract creation, we will take a closer look at the procedures of this process.

The above-mentioned purchase agreement is a standard contract of the Florida Bar, the Florida attorneys' association in Tallahassee. These contracts are created on the basis of the existing real-estate laws in Florida and in close connection with the federal laws of the United States. These contracts are fully formulated and contain open spaces in which the buyer's agent may insert the necessary contract details. These standard agreements may be accessed by any licensed real-estate professional in Florida for the conduct of their business.

A real-estate professional will not pass a copy of these standard contracts to a private individual because the real-estate expert is liable for handling errors in this case. Each copy of such a contract contains the name of the downloading agent and real-estate office.

The text passages in these standard agreements may be neither altered nor commented upon by a real-estate expert. If a real-estate professional makes changes to the agreement text, he or she is practicing legal counseling. Such an activity is illegal and will be prosecuted if the real-estate professional is not a licensed lawyer in Florida. This regulation applies in many other countries too.

In the blank space of the standard agreement, the buyer's agent puts in the names of the buyer and seller as well as their addresses. Further important details include the address of the property, the tax data, as well as the description, the location, and the size of the property. The agreement also needs information about the tangible items that will stay in the property and be included in the sale price.

The most important details of the contract are the purchase price and the earnest money on the purchase price. The purchase price does not necessarily correspond to the listing price. The buyer makes an offer to you, the seller, and this offer represents the price the buyer is willing to pay for your home. However, this price is always negotiable by both contract parties.

With the presentation of the offer, the first payment on the sale price is due. This deposit on the price should not be less than 10 percent of the purchase price; only then can you as the seller can be sure that the buyer is submitting a serious offer. With this deposit, the buyer binds himself to the contract. Should the contract be canceled in the future, then the buyer can lose this deposit, and you as the seller can receive the money. Details on this topic are explained in one of the following chapters.

In order to ensure that the deposit on the sale price is securely held for you and for the buyer, a title company is defined in the purchase agreement. This title company acts as trustee for all funds and performs the necessary settlement activities for a successful and clear transfer of the listing property.

Such activities include, for example, the investigation of the real-estate documents at the court, the public records, and the property information at the local municipality administration, as well as utility providers, such as water and power. The title company is also responsible for the deletion of existing liens.

The necessary documents for the transfer of the property from the seller to the buyer as well as the cost split in this transaction are calculated and processed by this service provider. More detailed information follows in one of the next chapters.

One important part in the sale agreement is the closing at a specific date. This date is normally thirty days after the date on which both parties have signed the binding contract. Before that date, all activities related to the agreement must be completed. All existing liens, open invoices, and possibly existing tax amounts due must be paid off from the sale revenue.

On the closing date, you, the seller, must have left your former home and handed over the keys to the new owner. In return, you will get the sale price after the deduction of all costs, commissions, and loans on your bank account.

A small note for you, Mr. Seller: if the purchaser of your home is not a cash buyer and needs a mortgage from a lender for a successful transaction, then the purchaser has to fulfill some information requirements during the transaction.

When you have signed the offer and the purchase contract is legally binding, then the buyer must immediately begin his mortgage-approval process for the purchase price with his lender. There is a timeline set for this activity in the standard contract.

According to the purchase agreement, the buyer must keep you informed about the progress of this activity. This does not mean that the buyer must tell you every little step, but the buyer must inform you in short notice whether he or she has been granted a loan in the required amount.

The buyer is obligated, with the delivery of the signed offer, to do everything necessary to get a mortgage approved for the sale price from his lender. If he does not, then he risks losing the earnest money, the deposit on the sale price.

The buyer will not lose this deposit if the lender cannot grant the loan due to the financial status of the borrower/buyer. In this case, the buyer may exercise the right to withdraw from the sale agreement with damage, and the earnest money will be refunded.

A small and very important tip for you: if the buyer offers you the entire purchase price as cash payment, then this is a good sign for you. In that case, the buyer does not have to go through the financing-approval process, and the risk that the contract will be canceled due to lack of mortgage approval is minimized.

In this case, you should still request at least 10 percent of the purchase price as earnest money and additionally request proof of funds for the rest of the purchase price. This is the only way to ensure that the buyer has the money to pay the sale price.

Another possibility for getting out of the sale agreement without losing the earnest money is a home inspection. The buyer has the right to inspect the property within a specific time frame, and if the results of this home inspection do not meet the expectations of the purchaser, he can withdraw from the binding contract without further justification. In this case the buyer gets his earnest money back in full. As a seller, you can only agree to the cancelation of the contract. More facts on this topic are explained in the chapter on the home inspection and its consequences.

In order to protect yourself against these unpleasant events in the sale process, you as the seller can request the right to sign a backup contract (replacement contract or second contract) from your buyer.

With such a backup-contract attachment, which is inserted into the sale agreement by your listing broker, the buyer grants you, the seller, the right to sign a replacement contract with a second buyer. However, this second contract remains invalid as long as the initial contract with the first buyer has not been terminated.

In the case of the backup contract, the earnest-money payment is only due when the initial contract is terminated and the backup contract becomes legally binding for the seller and the second buyer. As the seller, you have the assurance that you will be able to enter into the second contract immediately after the first agreement is canceled, and this second contract is the sale agreement that will close at the closing date.

There are a few more contract refinements that can improve your seller position, but these refinements are beyond the scope of this book and apply only in certain transactions. When you have further questions, you can send them to our e-mail address at the end of the book.

Let us now turn to your tasks, which start as soon as you have received an offer from a buyer and intend to accept this offer. As already mentioned, with your signature as a seller, the purchase contract becomes legally binding, and changes to this agreement are only possible in writing with the signatures of both parties.

Let us assume your house has a market value of $200,000, and you have received an offer in the amount of $180,000. This is just the purchaser's first offer. He is trying to get a favorable purchase price and wants to explore how much you would lower your price. The buyer does not expect that you will accept the first offered price, and his bid is only the opening price for the negotiations.

If this offer price is too low for you, then it is up to you to decide how you want to react to this offer. However, you should know your lowest acceptable sale price, and this price should cover all your costs and burdens from the real-estate transaction. You should close on this transaction with a black number in the sum line of the settlement statement. How big this black figure depends on the local real-estate market situation and how well your property conditions are in comparison to the other properties on the market.

Now we will look at your available options, how you can react and respond to the buyer's offer. This reaction will also be the beginning or the end of the negotiations in your transaction.

The possible options are these:

1.   You accept the existing purchase offer;

2.   You deny the purchase offer; or,

3.   You counter the purchase offer with a counteroffer.

Based on the offered purchase price of $180,000, we will examine your possible options and reactions to each option. Your listing price, which is based on the actual local market value, is $200,000, and that means there is a difference of $20,000, or 10 percent, that needs to be negotiated.

If you agree to the offer because your listing price was calculated on the higher end of the property market value, then you will sign the agreement and send it back to the buyer. With your signature, you have concluded a legally binding sale contract. Both parties, you and the buyer, can only withdraw from this contract within the terms and conditions that are written in the agreement document.

The second option is the rejection of the offer. You may send this rejection with the assistance of you listing agent to the buyer's agent without any justification. In this case, the purchase offer is not signed, and you cannot accept the deposit check for the earnest money. Both parties, you and the buyer, are free and untied and can enter at any time into another sale contract.

The third and last option is to counter the buyer's offer. In this option, you submit your own price offer to the buyer. For example, perhaps the $180,000 is not enough for you, and you want more; then you can ask for $195,000 in the counteroffer.

Your listing agent will then present that counteroffer with the modified purchase price to the buyer's agent. As you can see, your listing broker can help you with the unpleasant duty of delivering bad news, in this case, the changed higher purchase price.

If the buyer accepts the counteroffer with the increased purchase price, then you have a legally binding agreement. If the buyer does not agree with your counteroffer, then he has two options to react: to make a different new bid on your property or to end the contract negotiations.

When the buyer decides to stay in the negotiations, he will make a new bid. This bid will be between $195,000—our bid—and $180,000—his initial bid. The most likely amount for the new bid will be $190,000.

This sale-price negotiation will continue until both parties finally agree on one sale price or until one of the parties loses its patience, stops the negotiations, and signs a cancelation.

We will assume for demonstration purposes that you agree with the buyer on the purchase price of $190,000. This amended purchase price, accepted by both parties, is documented in writing on an additional document to the sale contract. When both parties have signed this additional document, it is inserted into the sale agreement and is legally binding, like the rest of the contract, for both parties involved.

After the negotiations on the terms and conditions of the sale agreement, the next steps in the real-estate transaction begin for all involved parties. For these next process activities, the contractually defined period is commonly thirty days.

Within this period, the necessary steps of the real-estate transaction must be completed; to such an agreement, the phrase "Time is of the essence" surely applies. If not all of the necessary measures are completed by the closing day mentioned in the contract, then each party of the contract has the right to withdraw and to cancel the contract. In such case, there is often a dispute about the earnest money amount and who will get it—the seller or the buyer. If there is no agreement on this issue, the court must decide who will get the earnest money or parts of it.

Let's return to our example:

You agreed with the purchaser of your home on a purchase price of $190,000. This agreement is reached on October 15, and the closing date of the transaction is scheduled for November 15, thirty days after the signing of the binding contract.

We will concentrate now on the necessary activities in this process. For the buyer, that means ordering the home inspector and applying for a mortgage if the buyer is not paying cash.

For you, the seller, further showings of your property are no longer necessary because you have a binding contract with a serious buyer. This buyer can only be released from the binding agreement under very limited conditions if he does not want to lose the paid earnest money.

However, you, the seller, are obligated to grant the home inspector access to your property. What this means to you in detail is explained in the chapter on the home inspection further down.

Another important task on your part is to cooperate with the title company that has been agreed upon in the contract. You have to ensure with your cooperation that the title to the property is transferred free and clear to the new homeowner. The title company is responsible for the examination of the property's public records and the preparation of all transaction documents up to the closing date. Details on these tasks are described in the chapter about the title company.

The Title Company Does Its Best to Ensure a Smooth Closing of the Transaction

While the buyer is busy working on his financing task and the arrangement of the home inspection, it is your job as seller to take care of the smooth preparation and handling of the sale documents.

Besides the purchase price, both parties have agreed in the contract to use a specific title company, ABC (this is a fictional name for this service provider for our example). This title company will perform the legal examination of the real-estate documents and will act as a trustee for the funds of the transaction.

To make sure that the following explanation does not confuse, here is a short description of what a title company does. The title company assumes some functions that are done in other countries by a special real-estate attorney. In Germany such an attorney is called a notary. This special attorney writes the contract for the sale of the property and examines the facts in the land registry and so on. In addition to these tasks, he also explains the legal details of the contract in a meeting to both involved parties—seller and buyer—and at the end of this meeting, both parties sign the contract with the attorney present.

In Florida the title company creates the necessary documents, but it does not provide legal advice to either party. For any legal counseling service, each party has to hire its own attorney and pay for the service. The hired attorney will explain the legal details to his client and advise on legal contract questions. But this legal service is performed separately from the closing.

The document, which represents the property rights on a specific property and lot, is called a "title" in the United States/Florida, and that is the reason for the name "title company."

In other countries—for example, in Germany—the attorneys are legally no longer allowed to act as trustees for funds and therefore may not handle the money within a property transaction. The funds are usually directly paid on the account of the involved transaction party.

In Florida, the title company assumes the task of a trustee. They collect and manage the funds within the real-estate transaction. The transfer of the funds from the trust account to the involved parties has to follow the legal regulations of the state.

When the offer was made, the purchaser of the property presented you with an earnest-money check—in our example, let's say $5,000—and this check was deposited with the buyer's agent office for safekeeping.

Now that you have signed the offer on the seller site, the purchase agreement is legally binding, and the earnest-money check is due. That means the buyer's agent office has to pass on the earnest money to the title company. The title company deposits the earnest money into its own trust account and sends you and the buyer a written receipt for this payment. This receipt can be sent by mail or e-mail, whatever you prefer, and is proof of the paid money.

If the agreed-upon total earnest-money payment is 10 percent of the purchase price, then the buyer has to deposit the difference between the first earnest-money payment and the 10 percent into the trust account of the title company at short notice. This payment can be done either by transfer or by check.

Let's come back to our example:

The purchase price of the property is $190,000, of which 10 percent is $19,000; we subtract the check amount of $5,000 that has already been attached to the offer. The earnest-money balance of $14,000 must be paid directly into the title company's trust account.

Besides the earnest money, the title company requires the seller's and buyer's information, such as name, home address, home country, telephone number, e-mail, and fax (if applicable), so that the real-estate documents for the new owner are prepared and issued correctly.

These personal data will be checked at the closing table when the involved parties sign the transfer documents. If you are a foreign-national property owner, you have to provide your passport.

In this context, both your real-estate professional and the title company will tell you that you are subject to FIRPTA, as a foreign national or alien.

FIRPTA is a US tax regulation. The sale of a property and the resulting sale proceeds are tax exempt within specific limits. The tax limits that currently apply are the following:

- For less than $300,000, no tax is due.

- For $300,000 to less than $1 million, the FIRPTA tax is 10 percent.

- For $1 million, the FIRPTA tax is 15 percent.

All citizens of the United States are responsible for the payment of any taxes themselves. However, in the past, foreign nationals often forgot to pay this tax, and therefore, the tax, whether it is due or not, is now deducted from the sale proceeds at the closing and passed on to the US tax authority.

You are the seller, and you can claim this tax amount according to the above limits when you file a tax return in the year following the sale of the property. Filing instructions are found on the website of the IRS, the tax authority, or you can speak with your tax accountant. We are happy to assist you with our business contacts if you send an inquiry to the e-mail address at the end of this book.

The next tasks of the title company are the review and investigation of all documents that are connected to the property, such as previous property transfers, real-estate tax payments, loans, and liens on the sale property.

To explain the differences between the land registries in Germany and in the United States, we'll take a brief excursion into the German land registry.

The most important document in this context is the land-register abstract. The important property details are summarized in that abstract. The land-register document consists of the inscription and the inventory as well as three sections.

The inscription of a land-register entry is the name of the respective property. This name consists of the municipality name as well as the volume/book and page number. It looks roughly like this: Register of Municipality Anywhere, vol. 12, page 3456.

The inventory of the property notes the exact address, location, and size of the buildings and plot, which are assigned to the above inscription with the volume and page number.

Section 1 contains the current owner of the buildings and piece of land as well as all the previous owners.

Section 2 describes the existing property rights and obligations associated with the land. These include right of way, rights for supply lines, right of usufruct, and more.

Section 3 lists the liens and loans on the property that result from existing or already repaid mortgages.

All these parts from the land registry together create the abstract of a specific plot and the buildings on it. The land registry is located in the district courthouse. Access to this abstract is limited, and you must prove a legitimate interest in the property to get this abstract. A legitimate interest is given, for example, when you want to acquire this particular property.

In the United States, there is similar documentation, but the terms are different, as are the filing and arrangement of the documents. The biggest contrast to Europe is that such real-estate facts are public records and can be reviewed by everyone.

The title document is called a "deed" and is issued by the court after the conclusion of the contract (the closing), and it is sent to the new property owner by mail. Additionally, this title certificate is archived in the public records at the district courthouse and can be examined online and printed as a copy at any time.

The inscription—that is, the name of the property—is a twelve-digit number in Florida. This ordinal number is used on all relevant documents and papers for this specific plot and property. That means that the respective documents are always connected to the specific property by the ordinal number. Besides the ordinal number, each document receives a book and page number, but this numbering depends on the creation date of each document.

The twelve-digit ordinal number is also used for the annual tax-assessment purposes of the property, and therefore, this number never changes. On the basis of this twelve-digit order number, it is possible to determine the physical location of the property in the county or region.

Let us now return to the title-company tasks. The title company collects all information about the former owners of the property and verifies that all prior ownership transfers were done properly and that all transfers were archived correctly.

In this context, there are two important property transfers to mention that often need higher attention at the title company: the property transfer within a probate proceeding and that within a divorce. For the probate transfer, the probate case must be completed before the property can be transferred, and during a divorce transfer, the property rights must be correctly adapted in the public records based on the divorce papers.

Documentation errors in the public records will lead to delays in closing preparations and cause issues with the title. Such a title is called "cloudy" or "dirty."

Such titles involve risks for the new owner and therefore require intensive processing and a solution for the issues. The transfer of such a title is only possible after the clearing of the issues, and the seller is required to assist in this clearing process and resolve the problems.

If you, the seller, do not cooperate in this matter, then the buyer of the property can sue you for "special performance," and that can become very expensive for you. In such a case, it is advisable to consult with a real-estate attorney and determine the best possible option to solve the issue. The title company will support you as much as possible; however, sometimes it will meet its business limits.

In the course of the title investigation, all public records and documents are searched at the court, listed, and subsequently checked to determine which liens and loans still exist and what the balances are. The title company determines which liens and burdens must be repaid and deleted before the transfer of ownership at closing.

The burdens and liens of a property in the United States include, for example, access to the power poles and water and sewage lines that are on the property or laid in the ground. These rights of use must be tolerated by each real-estate owner, just as it is the case in other countries.

The title company also checks whether all invoices for water and power are paid. If not, these open balances are to be paid by the seller at the closing. The buyer is responsible from the closing date for all these costs—in our example, this is November 15.

Further burdens on the property could be, for example, liens from a bank or lender. A lien is a security for a debt or mortgage that you have with a lender. Private loans, for example from a family member, are also registered as liens, and such a lien has to be repaid too by the seller before the closing.

Your task as the seller is to provide all the necessary documents, bank statements, and information if you have financed your property purchase in the past with a mortgage. The title company can also obtain the paperwork and the current balances from your lender; however, it will need a corresponding power of attorney from you.

The payoff of such a purchase loan is not a problem as long as you are not in financial distress, there are no payment arrears, and there are no foreclosure proceedings ongoing. In a financial-distress situation, there are intensive negotiations with the lender necessary to close on the property, and you have to participate and cooperate in these negotiations.

Such financial-distress negotiations are stressful and time consuming because your lender will lose money and would like to keep this loss as low as possible. These negotiations often result in delays for the scheduled closing date, and you must communicate these delays; otherwise, you can jeopardize the real-estate contract.

If you are taxable in the United States as a real-estate owner or as a professional, then tax liabilities can also lead to liens. Such liens must be paid off too before the closing so that the property is transferred without such liens.

In case you have not paid all invoices from handymen and contractors, then these persons will also put liens on the property that need to be removed before closing. The same applies to liens that have arisen in the context of curative treatments, or punishments imposed by your municipality because you have not complied with city codes, like mowing your lawn and cutting your hedges.

The title company verifies all of these liens and burdens and ensures that all known liens are permanently redeemed and deleted before the closing date.

As soon as the above tasks are done, a "title abstract" is created. This is a document of three to five pages in which the results from the title investigation are listed. This document is comparable to the land-registry abstract of many countries, and you, the seller, are obligated to check the correctness of the title abstract and to help solve any problems.

Based on the title abstract, the title is either free and clear, or it is dirty or cloudy. For a smooth closing, the title abstract should be free and clear.

These investigation results determine whether title insurance for your property is possible. Title insurance insures the property buyer against possible undetected, pending, or outstanding claims for which no documents are available in the public records at the time of the investigation. If title insurance is not possible due to existing title issues, then the buyer can reject the title and withdraw from the purchase contract.

Title insurance means the following to you: If a lien arises in the future for which you are responsible (and not the new owner), and this lien is put on the property, then the title insurance will take care of that issue. The title insurance will pay off the amount due and delete the lien; however, the title insurance will come after you for return of the paid money.

For a clean or clear title, title insurance is quick and easy to obtain. In the case of a cloudy title, only limited insurance is possible, while a dirty title is not insurable.

In the most cases, the costs for the title investigation and the title insurance will be paid by the seller. The costs are calculated on the property value and will be documented in the settlement statement at the closing table.

As soon as the title document—the title abstract—has been created, it is submitted to the buyer for review. This document must be completed and presented to the buyer in time, so he can decide whether the title is satisfactory.

As already mentioned above, the buyer can decide in the case of a cloudy or dirty title whether he will accept the risk of such a title or withdraw from the contract. Which decision is the best for the buyer, the buyer will certainly find out with his specialized attorney. Consulting with his attorney is an expense on the buyer's side and is not part of the closing costs. Therefore, these costs should not appear in the settlement statement at the closing.

If your buyer accepts a cloudy or dirty title, then the buyer cannot take recourse against you after the closing of the sale transaction, and the title insurance will only pay off liens that conform to the title-insurance agreement. For questions and details, the buyer must consult with a specialized lawyer to verify the risks of such a title. This book is only a guide to the process of the sale transaction and should not be taken as legal advice.

While the title company is engaged in the above tasks, you, Mr. Seller, have to be patient and participate in the title investigation and problem-solving process. Besides that, you also have to accompany the home inspector during the home inspection.

The Purchaser's Home Inspection—No Headache for a Prepared Seller

Besides the legal real-estate details, the purchaser has the right to a realistic impression of the structural building conditions of the new dream home. If you, the seller, have always maintained your property well, then this home inspection will not cause you sleepless nights.

When you signed the listing agreement with your listing broker, the agent probably asked you to complete and sign a seller disclosure. That is a document in which you have to disclose all known and important facts of your property—for example, when you bought the air-conditioning system, whether you made structural alterations inside or outside the property, and so on. This document is not mandatory for the seller, but it shows the buyer that you care for your home and know your home.

Regardless of this seller self-assessment of the property's condition, a smart buyer will order a home inspection on his expense to ensure that the building meets the purchaser's expectations. This inspection ensures that there will be no additional costs for the buyer shortly after the closing of the transaction that could have been deducted from the sale price before the closing. You will know what that means at the end of this chapter.

During such a home inspection, the inspector examines all important building and structural components of the property and documents his results in a report with appropriate photos for every examined item. Building and structural defects listed in this report give the purchaser the opportunity to cancel the purchase contract without any justification. In this situation, the buyer can reclaim the paid earnest money or can continue the contract to the closing and try to negotiate the purchase price based on the defects listed in the report.

On the other hand, such a home inspection can also be a benefit for you, the seller, because you can discover undetected flaws of your home. If you ask nicely, the buyer may provide you with the report. Based on this report, you can try to save the sale contract by showing yourself cooperative in fixing the home defects identified.

The most important points of such a home inspection are the condition of the roof, external walls, windows, and doors, as well as the electrical system and the in-house water system.

Within the framework of the inspection, the kitchen and the appliances included in the purchase contract are checked too. That means, in particular, that the refrigerator and the stove are tested for functionality and heating and/or cooling capacity.

For example, a dishwasher would be started and run through some cleaning program steps. The same applies to a washing machine and dryer, if they are included in the purchase contract.

The functionality and performance of the microwave oven, the hood, and the compactor under the kitchen sink are thoroughly tested and evaluated, as well as those of the hot-water heater and the air-conditioning system.

The home inspector will note type, description, and serial number of all appliances in the home and document this information in the report. With this report information, the buyer can check if your seller disclosure is correct. On the basis of the noted data, the home inspector can find out how old the appliances are, and the buyer can get an indication of when he or she will need to replace the appliances with new ones.

All household appliances that are sold with the property must be functional and must stay in the house when you move. You do not have to make any promises regarding the performance of the items, and you do not have to replace old equipment.

Any add-on features of the property, such as a pool, pool deck, automatic pool-cleaning system, backyard irrigation system, or private boat dock—if available—will be investigated too.

The next point on the checklist of a home inspection is the termite inspection. Many parts in a home are made of wood, and termites are Florida insects that love wood as their favorite food. The purpose of this investigation is to detect and identify termite infestation at an early state and protect the buyer from any costs arising from treatment. Such detection is also in the best interest of the seller because the buyer cannot come after the seller when an infestation is detected after the closing. Precaution and protection are always better than repairs afterward.

If the home inspector discovers a termite infestation, then the buyer has the right to request that the infestation be treated and has to pay for that treatment. However, the buyer cannot request the repair of any termite damage. The only option for the damage is to request a reduction of the purchase price.

In Germany, there are similar investigations in the real-estate sector for wood bugs, sponge, or mildew. Your home country will certainly have something similar too.

When examining the property documents, the home inspector also checks if all renovations and remodeling projects in your property have been done properly and with all necessary building permits. The city building inspector has to do a final inspection and declare the building project complete.

In the case of an open building permit, you, Mr. Seller, have a title issue that has to be resolved and closed out by the title company. The necessary activities in this context depend on the issue and the status of the building project. In such a situation, your cooperation is required to find a solution and move on to the closing.

The expenses for the home inspection are paid by the purchaser of the property, and these costs should not be listed in the closing statement.

Here is a little tip in regards to the home-inspection report, if you are able to get a copy from the buyer.

In the inspection report, the home inspector describes the deficiencies that he has identified, and he recommends a suitable solution for each issue. The costs that are mentioned for each issue are only estimations and can range from a few dollars up to thousands. The buyer will not know the actual expenses until he or she places a corresponding repair order to a building contractor. However, these projected buyer's costs are legitimate justifications to renegotiate the purchase price. If this renegotiation does not lead to the desired result, the buyer has the possibility to withdraw from the purchase contract.

If you, Mr. Seller, want to enter into the renegotiation of the purchase price and want to keep and close the contract, then you should think about which is the best way to achieve that goal. You have the option to remedy minor defects at your expense and keep the price as it is, or you can grant a reduction in the form of a dollar amount and let the buyer remedy the defects himself. Your real-estate professional will certainly help you, with his expertise, to make the decision that offers the biggest benefit for your transaction.

Here is an example for you to better understand:

Let us assume that your property has some small damage to the roof that has led to a dampening in one of the bedrooms. The damp damage is visible on the bedroom ceiling as spots. The exact cause of the damp damage is not known, and the home inspector is not allowed to investigate the damage by cutting open the ceiling and walls. The home inspector can only document the facts—moisture penetration—and give an approximate cost estimate based on his knowledge and experience.

In this case, the home inspector will examine the roof from the outside at the damage location, subsequently document his findings, and guess the cause based on his professional expertise.

This guess could be that the roof cover is damaged, letting water run into the home interior, damage the roof insulation, and cause the ceiling damage. The repair costs for this defect in our example are estimated at $300 to $1,000, depending on the actual damage cause and extent.

As a seller, you now have the option to have the damage repaired and not grant a discount on the sale price, or you can grant the buyer a discount of $300 on the purchase price.

With both options, you will probably be able to save the purchase agreement. In the first option, the purchase price stays the same, and in the second one, the purchase is adjusted with the written consent of both parties, and the transaction process moves on toward closing with a reduced price.

However, if you decide to do nothing—neither repair the damage nor discount the price—you will probably lose the sale agreement, and the buyer will get the earnest-money amount back.

Whatever you decide in such a situation, each decision must be in writing and signed by all parties. Verbal agreements or commitments are legally not enforceable and are therefore ineffective.

A period of five to ten days is stipulated for a home inspection in the purchase agreement. This time period is an integral passage in the purchase agreement, and the period starts when the contract is signed and legally binding for both parties, buyer and seller.

In our example, the start date for this period is October 15, and the end is ten days later. Before this end date, the purchaser must inform you if he is satisfied with the building status of the property and will stay in the contract, or if he wants to withdraw.

If the buyer does not perform a home inspection within the stipulated time limit, or if he renounces the inspection, then the purchaser accepts the property in the condition that he saw at the showing. In that situation, you as the seller are on the safe side, and the buyer has no right to withdraw from the sale agreement due to building defects.

In the event that the buyer nevertheless tries to withdraw from the sale agreement, then this is a breach of contract, and the buyer loses his earnest-money amount. When such a breach of contract occurs, it must be examined by a specialized real-estate attorney. Your listing broker cannot advise you or make that evaluation because that would be practicing law, which is illegal for a real-estate professional.

Let's Look for the Money—Cash or Financing from the Seller's View

If you think this chapter is not important to you because you are the seller, then you should think twice. This chapter is not about granting you a loan, but about the repayment of your existing loan.

Upon a second look, this chapter is clearly important—when does your buyer need a loan, and what kind of loan does the buyer want to get for the purchase of your home? This information, what kind of loan your buyer wants to get, is a part of the sale agreement, and you should deal with this point as much as your buyer does. Getting funding from a lender can cause delays in the closing process or can even lead to the cancelation of the sale agreement if the buyer lacks the necessary financial base to get the mortgage he needs to close the deal.

We'll start with a loan on your side and assume that you financed your property when you bought it. In this case, your loan agreement will most likely contain a repayment clause in the case that you sell the financed property. In such a situation, the lender usually allows the repayment without any prepayment penalties, even if you are still in the fixed-interest period. Therefore, you, the seller, should not see any additional costs in connection with the repayment of the loan in your column of the settlement statement at closing.

We do not know how such loan repayments work in your home country, but in Germany, you will almost certainly pay a penalty for the early repayment of the mortgage. This could get really expensive for you.

Until the big real-estate crash in 2008, you did not even have to repay the existing loan balance when you sold a financed property because it was possible to transfer the loan together with the property to the new owner under the terms of the mortgage agreement. The new real-estate owner then paid the monthly loan payment to the financing lender as the former owner did. The lender often did not know about this loan transfer because the lender did not have to approve the loan transfer.

This procedure was at that time legal and very widespread. The seller preferred this method because it was easy and inexpensive to pass on the property and the attached obligations and move on. There was only a small fee for rewriting and management, and the new borrower did not have to go through the whole lending and approval process.

This kind of loan transfer became problematic when the crash came and many borrowers became insolvent. At that time, foreclosure lawsuits were occurring on a large scale, and at times, 60 percent of the real-estate properties offered on the market were in some kind of distress. In the real-estate business, this is called "being underwater."

Because of the above-mentioned process of loan transfers, it was often difficult to connect the existing loan balance with the original borrowers and transferees so that the foreclosure process could be done legally and in the correct way.

Another difficulty was that many loan contracts had been sold for refinancing purposes to private investors on the market. Loan service and support had been outsourced to different companies. It was very hard to reconnect the borrower with the mortgage and the financed property.

Since the financial crisis in 2008, such practices are no longer practiced, and there are several new regulations in place that require the complete repayment of the loan when selling a financed property. The transfer of a loan contract is only ever possible with the consent of the lender, and the new borrowers must go through the lender's mortgage-approval process. Therefore, the advantage of this loan-transfer process is long gone.

For you, Mr. Seller, this means that you have to go through your loan documents with your lender and in cooperation with the title company to prepare them for the loan repayment and to clear the title of the mortgage lien.

In the repayment process, the title company assumes the task of managing and transferring the funds in the transaction. They receive the funds from the buyer on the trust account and pay the funds at the closing date to the lender. In return, the lender grants the deletion of the mortgage lien and sends the necessary documents to the title company, which passes these papers on to the court for execution. The related expenses to this procedure are paid by you, Mr. Seller.

Let us now turn to the buyer's payment options. Of course, it is always possible that your purchaser will pay cash. However, cash does not really mean cash in your hand. It simply means that your buyer does not need a mortgage and does not have to go through the financing-approval process. The cash payment is always welcomed by a seller. Nevertheless, for your own protection, you should always request an actual bank statement or a bank confirmation letter from the buyer that shows his financial status.

You also have to understand that the buyer cannot come to the closing with a briefcase full of money because that smells like money laundering. For that reason, your title company will also require the wiring of the funds to the company's trust account a few days before the closing.

In case of a cash payment that exceeds $10,000, the purchaser has to provide proof of where this money comes from. The title company will request this proof to ensure that this money is not so-called black money from crimes or drug trafficking, because the title company wants to protect itself from being charged with aiding and abetting.

If your buyer wants to pay with a bank-certified check, the equivalent of the funds must be received in the trust account of the title company at least two or three days before the closing date. Therefore, here's a small tip for you—contact the title company in time before the closing and make sure that the money has been received. That will help you avoid sleepless nights and frustrations.

Such money-laundering regulations also apply to Europe and many other countries in the world; however, there may be different cash limits and different evidence requirements.

Having reviewed your loan repayment and the cash-payment options in the sale transaction, let us take a look at your buyer's financing options.

Maybe you think it does not really matter where the money for the payment comes from. However, there are some financing options for the buyer that involve you in the process, and under some circumstance, you have to pay a part of these.

Let us start with the buyer's application for a loan to pay your sale price for the home. The purchase agreement specifies timelines in which the purchaser has to apply for a mortgage. If the buyer neglects these obligations and delays the transaction process, this can even lead to the cancelation of the purchase agreement, and the buyer can lose his earnest money.

Besides the usual real-estate financing loans with different interest rates and terms from bank institutions or private lenders, there are also mortgages provided or supported by government agencies. These loans are the FHA and VA loans.

In the case that the purchaser applies for an FHA loan, he can finance the sale up to 96.5 percent if his credit score is at least 580 points. In such a situation, however, you, the seller, are required to make some monetary concessions to the buyer.

For example, the equipment on the purchased property must correspond with government regulations. The structure of the building on the property must be in good condition so that no repairs are necessary before the buyer moves in. If this is not the case, you, the seller, must help out. You can either remedy the defects or give a discount on the purchase price so that the defect is repaired at your expense. Or it is expected that you will pay a concession toward the closing costs of the sale transaction.

A VA loan is only granted to veterans—active or former military personnel—who have at least a credit score of 620 points. In such a transaction, the real-estate property is financed up to 100 percent of the purchase price, but the home must to be in move-in condition. If this is not the case, such veteran financing will not be available for the veteran purchaser.

There is a limit on the seller's concession payment for an FHA or a VA loan, and that is 6 percent of the purchase price. If you accept a purchase offer in which the buyer intends to apply for an FHA or VA loan, you should keep this cost in mind.

Which terms and conditions apply to which type of loan and must be met is constantly changing. It is recommended that your listing broker get all the details and criteria for the loan together and discuss them with you before you accept the purchase offer. After the signing of the sale agreement, you no longer have any influence on this part of the deal, and you must fulfill the obligations of the contract.

The loan types—FHA and VA—may only be used as financing options if the buyer lives on the property, and the property is the buyer's primary residence. In case you know that the buyer is buying your property as an investment property and wants to finance this purchase with FHA or VA funds, then you must pass on this information to the title company. Otherwise, you may be held accountable for loan fraud if this is found out later.

Having reviewed the financing options that can influence your legally binding sale agreement, we will now look to further facts that can influence the real-estate transaction, including the appraisal. In many countries, this appraisal is done by the lending institution, but in Florida the appraisal is done by a specialized licensed professional. Such an appraisal is a property evaluation in connection with the loan process.

As already explained in one of the previous chapters, the listing broker determines the actual market value of your home, and you and your agent base your possible listing price on this market value. How such a local market value is calculated was described in one of the previous chapters.

However, this listing broker's market valuation is not the same as the appraisal. The appraisal evaluates the property from a different angle and is mandatory for the lender to determine how much of a mortgage can be offered risk-free.

In such an appraisal, the building structure on the property and its condition are, among other things, some of the most important criteria in the evaluation. The home inspection report that the buyer has already received from the home inspection can be included in this appraisal. In this report, the actual property status is documented with pictures. The individual building components as well as any deficiencies and possible repair work are presented and evaluated.

In the appraisal report, these up-to-date details about your property are combined with information on the construction method, property age, and any renovation, extension, and conversion measures. It calculates added values for add-ons, such as a pool, as well as discounts for wear and tear based on the age of the components and the building. The actual costs for the rebuilding of the property are estimated too.

The thus, the determined real-estate value of property will be compared with six equivalent homes that are within a radius of approximately one mile (1.6 kilometers).

Three of these comparable properties are listings. That means that these properties are actively offered for sale on the market, but they are not yet under contract. The remaining three properties are sale transactions that have closed within the last three to six months, calculated from the creation date of the appraisal.

These six comparable properties represent the current local market value of real estate in the direct neighborhood of your home. The agreed-upon purchase price of your property should be between 90 and 110 percent of the comparable property values. If that is not the case, then the purchaser will not get the necessary loan amount from the lender for the purchase, and that can create a problem for the transaction.

You may think that is not your problem, and to a certain point, you are right. If you have a backup contract (as already described above), or if the inventory on the real-estate market is very tight and the prospective buyers are lining up in front of your door, then you can be quite relaxed and wait to see what will come your way.

If this is not the case, then there are only two possibilities to save your legally binding contract with the buyer.

The first option is that the purchaser comes up with more money out of his pocket and covers the difference—whatever he will not get from the lender as a loan. In this case the sale transaction moves on without any interruption to the closing.

In the second option—if the buyer doesn't have enough money to cover the difference between the appraisal value and the purchase price—the buyer will ask you for a reduction of the sale price. You, Mr. Seller, have to decide if you want to agree on the price reduction or if you do not. If you want to reduce the sale price for the property, your listing broker will adjust the sale price in the existing agreement, and both parties—seller and buyer—have to sign this written attachment to the contract. The transaction moves on, with the reduced sale price, toward the closing after the signatures are given.

In case you do not agree on the reduced sale price, then the only option for both parties is the cancelation of the existing sale agreement. This cancelation must be in writing and signed by both parties, seller and buyer. After the cancelation, the seller has to return the earnest money to the purchaser.

In such a situation, there can arise disputes regarding whether each contract party has fulfilled its necessary obligations and who has caused the breach of contract. Each party will try to claim the earnest-money deposit for itself. To prevent an escalation, it is highly recommended that you seek the advice of a real-estate attorney in order to avoid court proceedings.

Neither the title company nor the real-estate professional is allowed to mediate in such a case; that would be illegal practicing of the law, which is certainly forbidden in your home country too.

Having explained the pitfalls of financing and title details, we will now return to our example of the sale transaction:

The average real-estate market value in your neighborhood is around $200,000.

All comparable real-estate properties are either slightly above or below the average value; they also have similar home and lot sizes and comparable features. This comparable evaluation results in a price range of $180,000 to $220,000 for the neighborhood in which your home is located. Your sale price in the binding real-estate agreement should be within this property-value range.

The earnest-money deposit—our example is $19,000, based on the sale price of $190,000 for your home—has already been received in the trust account of the title company. With this amount, you as the seller already have a share of the total sale price secured.

In our example, we assume that, based on the purchase price of $190,000, the lender will finance at least 70 percent of the sale price. That means the loan amount will be $133,000.

In this case, everything matches very well. The agreed-upon sale price of $190,000 equals 95 percent of the neighborhood market value. You've sold your property a bit beneath the market value; however, that means there's a solid financing base for your purchaser. The risk that the purchase agreement will be canceled is relatively low, and you can start to pack up your furniture, household, and private items.

If you have an outstanding loan balance from the purchase of your property, then by now, you and the title company will certainly have requested the necessary documents from your lender for the repayment of the loan and the deletion of the lien.

The loan documents from the lender will include a statement of the existing loan amount, including the interest payment until the closing date, as well as the necessary clearing and deletion papers for the liens on the property. These loan documents are a part of the closing papers and will be sent to the court for recording after the closing of the transaction.

The costs for the deletion of the liens and the recordings at the court are closing costs, which are the seller's expenses and will be listed in the closing statement in the seller column.

Congratulations!

You have now completed all necessary activities for a successful closing of your sale transaction, and you can now concentrate fully on moving out of your current home and looking for a new one.

Shortly before moving, you will have a visit from the new owner, your buyer, one more time, and that will be at the closing date. Information about this visit can be found in the chapter "Before the Closing—Activities of the Seller."

Difficult Issues That Have an Impact on a Real-Estate Transaction

The above description is based on common real-estate transactions without any special issues. However, you should at least know about a few of the most common special cases, because such special cases can influence the timing of a sale transaction.

Homeowners' or condominium-owners' associations

If your property is located in a homeowner community, the approval of the homeowner community, represented by the board, is mandatory for a real-estate transaction. A home can consist of a single-family home, townhome, villa, or condominium.

The reason the board's consent is necessary is that the homeowners' association in such a community owns the external facilities all together, and each member of the association has to pay a monthly maintenance fee.

Maintenance efforts are financed with these monthly maintenance payments. In order to ensure these monthly payments will occur, each owner has to prove his or her financial potential and commit to the agreed monthly payments. If you sell property in such a community, the homeowners' association loses a financially potent owner, and this owner should be replaced by a new financially potent owner. It is therefore a good idea that you give your buyer a little help to qualify for the homeowner community. This help is in your own interest as the seller; your buyer should make an excellent impression during the interview with the board to get accepted by the community.

As your listing agent will have informed you, you as the seller are obliged to provide the buyer with documents detailing the requirements of the homeowners' association. At the latest, after the signing of the binding agreement, these documents must be handed over to the purchaser for review.

These documents include community documents, the community rules and regulations, the most recent annual financial statements, the actual economic statement and the catalog of questions and answers about important association information.

After you've handed over the association documents, the purchaser legally has three days and no longer to review them and decide if he or she is willing to accept these binding association papers and the lifestyle of the community.

When these three days are over, the purchaser must inform the seller whether he or she intends to stick to the purchase agreement and close the deal.

In the case that the purchaser accepts the homeowners' association papers—your real-estate professional should request a written commitment note from the buyer and send this to you—then the sale transaction will be completed without interruption. The purchaser must now start the application process to get the approval of the homeowners' association, and as a first step, he or she has to pay the application fee.

If the purchaser fails to meet the above-mentioned three-day deadline, the documents are considered accepted. Canceling the purchase agreement based on the nonacceptance of the association documents and requesting the earnest-money deposit back are only possible within these three days. After these three days, any termination of the sale agreement will usually result in a dispute over the earnest money; the buyer will want the money back, and the seller will want to keep the money due to breach of contract. The buyer, then, should remember that time is of the essence; noncompliance with this deadline can be expensive for the buyer but mean money for the seller.

The above-mentioned application fees, which fund the background check of the buyer, are paid by the applying purchaser. This background check is expected to produce a negative result; hopefully the buyer has no criminal record, has not yet become delinquent, and has not filed for insolvency.

If the name of your purchaser appears in any database that is reviewed during the background check, the review will be positive.

The review information is only communicated to the homeowners' association and the board members and is not shared with you, the seller. You will only get a denial letter from the association with no rejection details.

To save your sale transaction in such a situation, it is best to have an open conversation with the buyer and try to find out what the issues are with the background check. The homeowners' association must tell the purchaser why the application has been rejected, and then you can work on those problems.

Perhaps the buyer's name was simply mixed up with another person's, or maybe there was a mistake in the databases. The buyer should check for erroneous data and have them corrected; such data can have serious consequences in the future if not corrected.

If it turns out that the reason for the denial is not in accordance with the Fair Housing Act, the purchaser should file a complaint with governmental authorities. Unreasonable or wrongful discrimination toward a protected group of persons is a federal criminal offense and is prosecuted by the federal governmental agency. A complaint filed in a timely manner can therefore save your real-estate deal if the purchaser is still interested in buying the property despite the refusal by the homeowner community.

We can assist you in determining how and where to file such a complaint against the offender. For more information, you can use the e-mail address at the end of the book.

In our example, we will assume a negative background check result and that your buyer will be asked to come to a personal interview as a new co-owner. This interview is an informal introduction between the homeowners' association and your purchaser. The participants are the current homeowner representatives—the board—and your buyer, the future owner.

At the end of the interview, your purchaser will be issued a certificate indicating the approval of the homeowners' association and showing that your buyer is accepted as a new member of the homeowner community. This document is an important paper within the closing documents and must be available on the closing date at the title company; otherwise, there will be no closing.

Short-sale transactions

The content of this book is meant as a guideline for a real-estate seller in Florida or the United States. We assume that you, the seller, are in a financially safe position and not in a distressed situation.

To complete this topic, we will briefly explain the term "short sale," what such a situation means for a seller, and what its effects are on the course of a real-estate transaction. These effects are different but unpleasant for both contracting parties, purchaser and seller.

In such a situation, the real-estate seller or owner has struggled with financial issues. The seller is still the owner of the property and must meet the obligation to pay the monthly loan payments. However, if the property owner loses his job or cannot work due to sickness, he will not be able to fulfill this obligation and will fall behind.

Under the terms of the loan agreement, the lender is entitled to terminate the loan agreement after two outstanding monthly payments, and in that case, the lender will request the entire loan amount back. This procedure is called "lis pendens," and it initiates the foreclosure process.

When the bank has terminated the loan agreement and has initiated legal action, it often allows the seller to find a suitable purchaser for the property. This procedure is called a "short sale," and it has many benefits for the lender and the borrower.

With his cooperation in this procedure, the borrower (the seller of the property) can be relieved of any residential debts that may remain after the short-sale process, and the loan repayment will not appear as a foreclosure in the borrower's credit history. A foreclosure auction and its related consequences will affect the seller's credit score for at least seven years, while a short-sale process will allow a new real-estate loan after twenty-four months.

However, in the case of a short sale, a real-estate professional must be entrusted with the marketing of the property; a real-estate professional will achieve better sale success due to his better technical marketing tools. When the marketing is done by a real-estate expert, the property appears on more than one thousand national and international real-estate portals and reaches billions of potential buyers. As a result, sale opportunities increase enormously.

In addition, the lender wants to prevent the property from being sold to a family member of the borrower or to be sold at a very low price through unfair practices to a speculator. It is in the best interest of the lender to obtain the highest possible sale price because that will minimize the loss for the lender and make it easy to forgive the deficiency.

When the property is offered on the market and a purchaser is found, the seller and the purchaser conclude a binding sale agreement. This sale contract is submitted to the lender for approval.

No lender wants to lose money, and therefore, intensive negotiations between seller and lender are necessary. In these negotiations, topics include not only the sale price of the property as listed in the agreement but also the amount that the seller/borrower will have to bring to the closing table or that will be forgiven at the closing. If these negotiations are successful, the seller will not only sell the property but also be debt-free after the closing.

Negotiators under these circumstances are usually tenacious, which can lead to delays on the path to the closing. In this case, the property buyer is expected to have a little patience. The buyer and the seller should expect a time frame of between 90 and 180 days.

For this patience, however, the purchaser receives a well-maintained property because the seller is responsible for and must maintain the property as long as he is the owner. Additionally, the buyer will get transferred a free and clear title at the closing.

Short sales were a big issue during the burst of the real-estate bubble and the years after, but today, short sales are no longer a problem.

Bank-owned and deed-in-lieu properties

The third special case involves bank-owned real-estate properties. These are in the ownership of a lender, and they are offered on the market for sale as "real-estate owned" or REO, also known as bank owned. In such a situation, the lender has already completed the foreclosure process on these properties.

These properties are often offered below the actual market values of their local neighborhoods, but the building conditions of these properties are mostly not very attractive. In such a home, the former owner has left some time ago, and these properties are rarely rented by the lender. The owner of the property is the lender, and it maintains the home with only limited effort to ensure code compliance to avoid fines for neglect. The titles of such properties are not always clean and clear.

For a deed-in-lieu property, this is somewhat different. In this case, the former homeowner leaves the home voluntarily and without going through the court proceeding of a foreclosure. When the former owner moves out of the home, the lender and the owner enter into an agreement in which the lender receives the keys to and all rights of the property. In return, the existing loan, which is already in default, is repaid without the judicial foreclosure, and the borrower is released from all his obligations. Nevertheless, it is recommended that you have this agreement with the lender reviewed by a special real-estate attorney to ensure that the agreement is favorable for you, the owner.

The title of such a deed-in-lieu home is often much better and cleaner than the title of a court-foreclosed property, where title issues are not cleared.

With the conclusion of this deed-in-lieu transfer of the property, the homeowner is debt-free. Such a process has a smaller impact on the homeowner's credit score than a completed foreclosure of the home. This procedure is not a regular sale because there is only one buyer—the lender—involved. This is only a possible option, and its explanation is intended to complete the scope of this book.

Before the Closing—Activities of the Seller

We based our example on a regular, common sale transaction, and such a transaction normally closes within thirty days. By now, these thirty days are almost over. You, Mr. Seller, have taken care of the repayment of your loan, if that was necessary. You've also supported the title company with the necessary title investigation and cleanup of existing title issues. The finish line—the closing—is near enough to grasp.

You probably also had a clarifying meeting with your tax accountant to discuss the issue of the FIRPTA tax, including what the process is and how you can proceed in the best way.

It is often suggested that you request a certificate from the tax authority in order to avoid the tax payment at the closing. Here is a small note based on many years of practice in the real-estate business: you will not get this certificate in 99.9 percent of cases because you will not have all documents necessary for this kind of certificate. Besides that, many title companies are afraid that the tax authority will come after them if the certificate has been wrongfully issued. Therefore, the title company will insist that you, the seller, pay your tax and file a tax-return claim with the tax authority the year following after the sale.

Let us examine this point a bit from the seller's point of view. This description is based on our own experience and does not replace professional tax advice; every sale situation is different and must be treated differently.

As already mentioned, the foreign-national seller must pay a 10-plus percent FIRPTA tax to the US tax authority at closing. However, this tax is refundable when you file for a tax return and when your sale proceeds are below $300,000.

The tax amount due based on the purchase agreement is sent by check and with a cover letter from the title company to the responsible tax department. When this check has cleared, and after processing the tax payment, the seller will receive a receipt letter from the tax authority approximately two or three months later. This receipt also contains details about the sale transaction, such as the buying and selling dates, the purchase price, and the property address.

When you have received this voucher, you can apply for a tax ID number using a copy of this voucher and a copy of the closed sale contract as well as a notarized copy of your ID papers. The tax number is required for your later tax-return filing.

After you get your tax number, you can download the necessary tax documents from the IRS (Internal Revenue Service) website and complete the form. All documents, including a certified copy of your identity card or passport, must be sent by mail to the relevant IRS department of the United States of America.

If all documents are completely and correctly filled out, and if you are eligible for a return claim, then you will receive your tax amount back by check, usually with accrued interest.

That is the usual way. Let us now turn to the topic of the tax certificate and why that procedure does not work. You need a US tax number to be issued a certificate, but you will only get a tax number when the tax has already been paid and the real-estate contract has been settled in full. The goal of this certificate is to avoid the unnecessary tax payment; however, this is impossible due to the above-mentioned criteria for a certificate.

Perhaps you are thinking, "I have a social security number, which is also used as a tax number in the United States." That is very nice, but it will not help you; the social security number is not accepted in this case, and you will not get a tax certificate. Just accept that you have to pay the FIRPTA tax payment and ask for a refund later.

Another step you must take before the closing day is to move out of your sold property. It is a good idea neither for you as the seller nor for the buyer if you stay in the property beyond the closing. In such cases, it is almost certain that there will be a dispute later about damages inflicted while you were living there or when you moved out. And we will not even talk about possible rent-payment disputes; those often arise too.

As you know from your property ownership period, you have to pay the annual property tax. This tax amounts to approximately 2 percent of the actual property value, without the consideration of possible tax reductions due to market-price fluctuations or the so-called homestead (tax deduction for the primary residence).

Until the closing date, you are the responsible homeowner of the property, and you are responsible for the tax amount, even if the amount is not yet due.

Property tax is calculated from January 1 to December 31, but it is due only after the tax invoices are issued and sent out to the property owners at the end of October or the beginning of November each year.

Depending on who receives the tax invoice—purchaser or seller—that person must pay the total amount of the property tax. However, in the closing statement, this tax amount has already been split on a day-by-day basis between both parties, and the calculated tax amount is included in the column of the relevant party. You will find details on this topic in the chapter about the closing statement further down in the book.

For clarification purposes, here is an example calculation illustrating how you can reckon your property-tax share. We use the same numbers from our real-estate transaction that have already been used throughout the book.

In the year of the property sale, your tax is, for example, $4,000. However, you only owe the portion of the tax that is due for the period from January 1 to the closing day. The purchaser is responsible for the time from the closing day to the end of the year. As part of the closing statement for the sale transaction, this tax amount is divided between the seller and the buyer, proportionately, for the current tax year.

As already mentioned, the closing day is November 15, and from that date, the buyer must pay the property tax.

The bill with the tax amount for the current year is sent out at the end of October or at the beginning of November, and you can only pay your tax when you have the bill and know the exact amount on that invoice.

In our example, that means that the purchaser has to pay the total tax amount; however, you have to credit your share of the tax amount in the closing statement. You will next see how that works.

Our example calculation looks like this:

Annual tax amount = $4,000

Tax divided by calendar days = $4,000 / 365 = $10.96 per day

Seller share from January 1 until November 14 = $10.96 x 318 = $3,485.28

You, Mr. Seller, will pay to the buyer your tax amount of $3,485.28, and the buyer will pay the total sum of the real-estate tax of $4,000 to the county's tax department at the due date. With the credit to the buyer, your tax amount is settled.

We certainly do not have to tell you that you have to pay your water, waste water, and power bills until the closing day. In order to prove your payment, you should send the payment receipt of the outstanding balance to the title company. If you do not, the open balance amount will be deducted from your sale proceeds, and the title company will pay the invoices for you.

Now you have completed all the necessary activities, submitted all the requested documents, discussed all your open questions with your personal experts—attorney, tax consultant, and so on—and there is nothing blocking your way to your successful closing.

The last countdown starts to run, and at least forty-eight hours before the closing, you must get the complete set of closing documents for review as well as the closing statement. You have to examine these papers closely and clarify any open issues and errors because it will be too late to do it on the closing date, when you sign the papers.

When all documents are correct and no errors are found in the closing statement, then you only need your keys. You have to bring the keys with you and hand them over to the purchaser when the closing papers are signed. In exchange, you will receive the sale proceeds, which were calculated in the closing statement, into your bank account. You will not get any cash money at the closing table because that is illegal.

Finally—Closing the Transaction

You did it! The big day of closing your real-estate transaction has come. You have received the time and location for the signing of all real-estate documents. You are certainly glad to have finally reached the end of your sale transaction and to have finished all other expenses.

One final task is still open, and that is the last walk-through of your former home. During this last walk-through, the buyer has to check that the seller has moved out. You, Mr. Seller, should be present at this walk-through, create a document about this activity, and sign it together with the purchaser. You certainly do not want to hear later that you damaged the property while moving out or that you took any tangible property that was sold with you. Such discussions can torpedo the subsequent closing, and that is not your intention—right?

Such a walk-through usually takes place immediately before the closing. Subsequently, after this passage through the home, the parties meet at the title company's conference room for the signing of the closing papers.

The closing agent of the title company welcomes both parties, seller and buyer. This closing agent is, in many title companies, a real-estate attorney or someone with corresponding training in the field of closing who can answer your questions in regards to the papers. However, this closing agent will not conduct any legal counseling during the closing.

The closing agent is an employee of the title company and is not a representative of the closing parties. During the closing process, the agent explains all documents provided by the title company and answers questions raised about the information within the documents. Besides that, the closing agent checks the identifications of the seller and the buyer and certifies during the closing the signatures of the parties on the papers.

Often, real-estate professionals also come to the closing and participate in it. This is not mandatory, but it is the final touch of your real-estate professional to the transaction.

As a real-estate broker myself, I think it is appropriate to be involved in the closing. It is the icing on the cake of all the hard work of the transaction, and your real-estate professional will receive the payment for that hard work immediately after the closing.

When all transaction parties are present and welcomed, the closing agent explains the different documents and where the documents must be signed.

Each signature of either party must be notarized by the closing agent. With this certification, the documents become legally valid. This public-notary seal corresponds to the certification by a special attorney in Germany. You will certainly know how that works in your country.

It is common for all documents to be available multiple times, and each must be signed in person. Copied signatures are often not allowed for recording in the public records. However, this process could change in the future for environmental reasons.

The seller and the buyer will each receive an original stack of papers; one original will remain with the title company; one original will be filed with the remaining documents at the court; and if there is a lender involved, one original will be sent to the lender. The participating brokerage offices will receive a copy together with the commission checks.

After all documents are signed and certified, the keys of the property are handed over, and the funds in the trust account of the title company are paid out based on the signed closing statement. Then the closing is finished, and all parties are on their way.

In our example, we assumed that all parties were on the spot during the transaction closing. However, there is also the option that you, as the seller, could perform a closing in absence. This is also possible on the buyer's side.

In such a case, the documents will be sent by mail to you, the seller. When you have received the documents, you must go with the entire paper stack to the nearest US embassy or consulate. There, each document must be signed at the marked spot, and a US official must certify each performed signature. Subsequently, all signed documents will be returned to the title company for further processing. In this case, the money and the keys are exchanged when the signed and certified closing papers arrive back at the title company.

The Transaction Statement

Let us return to the closing statement. A form for the closing statement is provided by the US Department of Housing and Urban Development (HUD) and is also known as the RESPA statement (Real Estate Settlement Procedures Act).

The purpose of this closing statement is to protect the consumer and to avoid the invoice slowly dripping over months, as is happening in Germany.

We have sold several real-estate properties in Germany and have mainly handled these transactions from abroad, so we know what we are talking about. When we've negotiated and signed the sale contract in absence, we've received the sale proceeds five to six weeks after the contract's signing. After the signing, the invoices for fees and charges arrived over three to six months from various institutions and professionals. This delayed the completion of the real-estate transaction significantly, and it was difficult to keep an eye on the actual related costs of the transaction.

In the United States, there is only one settlement statement on the day of the closing, and this settlement is final. An original version of this statement is extensive and confusing, so it is not suitable for presentation in this book. Therefore, we'll only show a simplified version based on the Broward and Miami-Dade County requirements.

If your property is located in a different county than Broward or Miami-Dade, your settlement statement at the closing will differ in some closing-cost positions.

The schematic statement form lists all fees and expenses related to the sale transaction that are paid by either the seller or the buyer. The expenses shown in the statement are also listed in the purchase agreement. By signing the purchase agreement, both parties define the cost allocation, and this expense allocation becomes an important part of the sale agreement.

After the closing, all legal activities are completed, and you as the former owner of the property do not have to expect any further expenses.

Example RESPA statement

Single-family home

Three bedrooms/three bathrooms/one garage

Cash transaction for $190,000

Closing date—November 15

Settlement	Buyer	Seller
Sale price	-$190,00.00	$190,000.00
Commission to the real estate agents (6 percent)		-$11,400.00
Tax for 2016 (total = $4.000,00)	$3,485.28 a)	-$3,485.28
Title search		-$90.00
Lien search		-$225.00
Title insurance	-$1,025.00	
Closing service	-$525.00	-$585.00
Doc stamps 0.70 percent per $100		-$1,330.00
Deed recording	-$27.00	
FIRPTA tax (10 percent based on sale price)		-$19,000.00 c)
Total sum to pay to the seller	-$188,091.72	$153,884.72 b)

a) Credit annual tax share, seller to buyer
b) Payment sale price to the seller
c) Claim from the IRS in the tax year following the sale transaction

Let us now look at the individual items on the statement. In order to clarify the principle of the statement and to keep it simple and comprehensible, a cash transaction has been selected and used.

The inclusion of the loan payment on the buyer's side and the repayment of an existing loan on the seller's side would only complicate the closing statement and does not provide any additional insights into the principle.

As already mentioned, as the seller, you pay the commission in the sale transaction. When you signed the listing agreement with your real-estate professional, you agreed on the commission rate and the commission that will be due when the property is sold. The usual commission rate is 6 to 7 percent of the contract amount. This commission is due and must be paid as soon as the sale transaction has closed. The actual commission amount is calculated based on the actual sale price and not the listing price, and the amount is deducted from the sale proceeds before the seller gets the money.

The listing agreement also stipulates that the commission is to be shared with a cooperating agent. The cooperating real-estate professional is the buyer's agent. If the listing broker has to work with both parties, buyer and seller, the listing agent becomes a transaction agent, and the entire commission amount is paid to the listing office.

With this commission, the services of your listing broker in connection with the sale transaction are paid for, as already stated in the chapter about the tasks of the real-estate professional.

However, if your listing broker has provided additional services, such as the translation of documents, this service has to be paid separately.

The next item on the settlement statement is the property tax; the shares of the seller and the buyer are listed in the corresponding columns. The property tax and the payment are due in November each year, and the tax amount is split exactly at the closing date.

Here are the calculations for our example:

The total annual property tax is $4,000 ($200,000 x 2 percent = $4,000). The closing is done on November 15.

This means the following:

The year has 365 days; from January 1 to November 14, we have 318 days. The tax amount for this period is $3,485.28.

The calculated tax amount is the tax liability of the seller for the current year. By the due date, you, the seller, are unlikely to have any more connection to the buyer, and a partial tax payment is technically not possible. Therefore, you, the seller, pay your share of the tax to the buyer within the sale transaction, and this amount will be stated as a credit to the buyer in the settlement statement at closing.

The closing expenses that you, the seller, usually pay are the costs for the title search and the lien search. These examinations of the property documents make sure that there are no restrictions or liens at the time of closing and that the title is transferred free and clear.

This document review is the prerequisite for obtaining title insurance in an unrestricted or restricted form. Details on this topic are included in the chapter about the title company and its services.

For the title and lien searches, there is usually a flat rate or flat fee to pay. Only in very urgent cases—for example, when the sale transaction should close in fewer than thirty days—is an additional fee for the express handling required. The regular runtime for a title search and a lien search is different from municipality to municipality, but it cannot be done in less than two or three weeks.

The next item in the closing statement is the title insurance. Expenses for the title insurance are commonly paid by the purchaser because this insurance benefits him or her.

Title insurance covers the risk that there may be a potential claim against you, the seller, that is not yet recorded in the public records and was therefore not discovered during the title search. Such an undiscovered claim can become a lien after the closing. In this situation, the title insurance pays this lien off and orders the deletion of the lien. If you, the seller, are responsible for this lien recording, then the title insurance will come after you and take recourse to obtain the money.

The processing fee is paid for the title company's preparation of the necessary real-estate-transfer documents, like copying, mailing to the court, and so on. Both parties have to pay for these services because both seller and buyer receive corresponding work. The services for the seller are usually more intensive and more complex, and therefore, the seller's expenses are higher than those of the buyer.

The deed is the property certification. This document shows who the seller is, who the buyer is, what price the property sold for, and on which day. For this deed document, the seller must pay the doc stamps. This expense is calculated based on the purchase price—in our example, 0.7 percent per hundred dollars of the purchase price.

In our example, the sale price is $190,000, meaning $1,330 in document-stamps costs for the seller.

The position survey—the measurement of the land and the buildings—should only appear in the settlement statement if the buyer has commissioned the title company to obtain a survey. The cost for the survey must be paid by the buyer and should be listed in the buyer's column.

In the United States, there is no central authority for the measurement of properties like there is in Germany. Therefore, each real-estate owner has to hire a land-surveying company to get the correct perimeters of your property. Since this book focuses on the sale transaction, this topic will not be discussed in detail, and this cost item does not appear in the closing statement. The example found here is included only to round up the topics described in this book.

The item "recording deed" refers to the expense of registering the transfer of ownership from the former owner to the new owner. This cost is a lump sum from the court (comparable to the district courts in Germany).

In our example sale transaction, we assume that you, the seller, are a foreign national—not a US citizen—and are subject to the FIRPTA tax when selling your property. The details of this tax were already explained in one of the preceding chapters, and we have deducted the tax amount of 10 percent from the sale proceeds. This amount can be refunded by the tax authority if you, the seller, are eligible for it and file a tax claim the year following the sale.

In the sum line, you will find two respective amounts—what the buyer has to pay in total and what the seller will find in his bank account after the deduction of all transaction costs.

Congratulations!

You have now successfully sold your home and handed over the keys to the new property owner, and the sale proceeds are on their way into your bank account.

You have successfully realized your goal of conducting a property sale in a foreign country.

WHAT IS NEXT?

That depends on the desires and objectives that you set before the sale of your home. If you sold your property because you need a bigger one due to family growth, you can now search for the new one. The same applies if you want to move into a smaller home. Perhaps your children moved out, left to study at a college or university, or got married and want to have their own families.

If you sold your home because you have a new job at a different location, then you can start on your way into that new future.

If you had a divorce or inherited the sale property, then it is time to close this chapter and decide where you want to go next. Leave everything behind that connects to your former home, and look to the horizon, where the next destination is waiting for you.

If you sold your property because of a financially distressed situation in the form of a short sale or a deed-in-lieu transaction, you should definitely consult with a lawyer and tax consultant so that the forgiven loan amount is not mistakenly declared as income in the tax filing. You will need a special paper from your lender as proof that the loan has been forgiven. This is just well-intended advice, but you certainly know—caution is better than forbearance.

If the home you sold was a vacation or second home, it is time to think about what you want to do with the sale proceeds. As long as you and the money stay in the United States, this decision is easy to make: first, put the money into your bank account, and then invest it in new assets—perhaps a new property in another location. We can help you with your search, your move, and all other matters, wherever you want to go. Send us an e-mail at the address at the end of the book, and we will be at your side, worldwide.

When you want to leave the United States and move back to you home country, then you should take a moment and think about the necessary steps. There may be some issues to consider when transferring the money back home due to legal regulations.

Each foreign country usually has rules and regulations regarding how much money you can transfer from abroad to your home country and which reporting forms you need to use. For transfers of large money sums, you will have to prove where the money has come from; otherwise, your home-country authorities may suspect money laundering, and that is a criminal offense in many countries worldwide. However, your transaction documents should be good evidence in such a situation, or your tax accountant can give you valuable advice on how to handle this matter.

Please ask yourself, before you transfer all the funds to your home country and close all accounts in the United States— are there any open expenses that must be paid, or do you expect any further income?

For example, if you've sold an inherited property, you should check if you must pay inheritance tax. Also, the probate process—the inheritance process in the state of the United States where the inheritance occurred—must be fully settled. Probate procedure causes costs that must be paid in US dollars, and if your money is already back home, you will have to wire it from home and buy dollars at the actual currency rate. These rates are constantly changing and can be negative for you.

Another consideration before you close your account should be the possible FIRPTA tax refund. This tax refund is paid in US dollars and can be made either as an account transfer or as a check. If you do not have an account in the United States anymore, your only repayment option for the tax is a check.

This check is issued in US dollars and must be deposited into an account in your home country in the absence of a US account. In this case, the currency conversion and the handling charges are not cheap and can quickly add up to a bigger amount. Banks are very innovative when it comes to requesting fees and charges from their customers, especially in today's economic situation.

To keep the costs of the currency conversion in control, there are several legal, trustworthy service providers that can help you. These service providers ensure a problem-free transfer of larger amounts of money and also offer the possibility to profit from the exchange rate. If you are interested in more information, please send an e-mail to the e-mail address at the end of the book, and we will be happy to help you.

A LAST WORD AT THE FINISH LINE

You have successfully sold your home—at least in this book. With a local real-estate expert, your experience will certainly be easy and relaxed. If you have familiarized yourself with the real-estate sale process by reading this book, you will be a good partner to your real-estate professional for sure.

In reality, you will feel much better. You will at last have the money from the sale transaction in your bank account, and all obligations related to your former property will be paid and ended—no more monthly loan payments, no more monthly maintenance charges or property costs, no more real-estate taxes.

If you bought your property at the low point of the real-estate market, then you will have also realized a really nice profit on the sale of your home.

The local economy has recovered very well since the real-estate bubble in 2008 and the decline of property values by 2011. At that time, real-estate values had fallen to 40 percent of their values before the bubble, and many property owners had big financial problems and could hardly pay their monthly loan payments. There were many short sales and foreclosure sales, which flooded the real-estate market and thus led to the extreme decline of market values in real estate.

However, it was already apparent at that time that these real-estate values would recover quickly. Not only did the improvement in the local economic situation provide relief, but the local ecology also contributed.

Governmental subsidies have created new jobs, and structural measures have attracted new investors and businesses to the region. With these investments and structural measures, employee numbers have increased, and these employees need housing, which has to be constructed. Now the metro region of Miami/Fort Lauderdale is booming again and is one of the top business, trade, and tourist destinations in the United States.

Florida is a peninsula, and large parts of the southern tip of this peninsula consist of the nature reserve of the Everglades. This conservation area is vital to the region and greatly limits the expansion and development of the metro region of Miami and Fort Lauderdale. New construction projects can only be realized within the currently available perimeters of the region, and therefore, the real estate that is created within this limited area will continue to rise in value.

This development of property values is also demonstrated by the following static figures, statistics based on the last eleven years in the metro region of Miami/Fort Lauderdale.

Market research since the burst of the real-estate bubble shows that the average losses in real-estate values were 50 to 60 percent in 2008. The real-estate market reached its lowest point in 2011, and the market values initially rose slowly. In 2016, the former peak values were exceeded, and they are still increasing.

Besides these developments in real-estate values, you also should not forget the exchange rate movement during this period. Even though the dollar got stronger over the years, the currency rate between the US dollar and the euro is still beneficial for a European. The exchange rates fluctuated between $1.06 and $1.50 to €1.00 during the period of the study. This means that, with a conversion rate of $1.25 to €1.00, if you buy a house worth $200,000, you will only pay about €160,000.

Statistics about the real-estate values for the last eleven years are as follows:

Single-Family Home in Fort Lauderdale (Average Sale Price)			
	Basic	With Pool	With Waterfront and Pool
2005	$204,870	$322,555	$531,808
2008	$119,509	$133,948	$146,761
2011	$100,085	$214,731	$408,226
2014	$150,718	$245,511	$445,146
2016	$252,519	$416,652	$733,976

To make these numbers a little bit more understandable, here is a specific example:

Let us assume that you bought a real-estate property in Florida on April 14, 2011. This home cost you $200,000, and the exchange rate of US dollar to euro was $1.45 to €1.00.

Based on these data, for this specific real-estate property, you only had to pay about €137,931 ($200,000 / $1.45 = €137,931.03).

Now let's say that on November 15, 2016, you sold this exact real-estate property. In this example, we are not considering any renovations, modernizations, or annual holding costs; we are limiting ourselves to the selling price only.

Due to the rise in real-estate property prices, you can now sell your property on the market for twice the purchase price. In this specific case, you can sell your home for $400,000.

As you certainly know, the conversion rate of the US dollar to the euro is currently almost equal. On November 15, 2016, the rate was $1.07 to €1.00. If we take this rate into account, then you would get around €373,832 for the sale price of $400,000.

When we start with a capital investment of €137,931, then you get back €235,901 now, after approximately five and a half years. Again, this profit is based solely on the property's increase in value and leaves costs, interest payments, or maintenance out of consideration.

These property-value increases are also listed in the table above. As the basis for this statistics study, only Fort Lauderdale properties that were actually sold by a local licensed real-estate professional in Florida were used.

As the figures impressively show, the real-estate values have risen differently in various segments. Among basic properties, which have neither a pool nor a waterfront, the value increased by 152 percent; for properties that have both a waterfront and pool, the value increased by only about 80 percent.

It goes with saying that these figures are based on the assumption that you entered the real-estate market and bought a property near the low point of the market and that you're leaving the real-estate market today.

You will only achieve such numbers and profits if you hire a competent, licensed real-estate expert in Florida. This professional will be a reliable partner for you in your real-estate business and will use his knowledge and expertise to your advantage.

You should not make the mistake of believing, after reading this book, that you can manage a real-estate transaction on your own. The purpose of this book is to give you an overview of a common and simple sale transaction. All data and details presented in this book were valid at the time of the book's creation, but they may change at any time due to new laws and regulations.

Each property and transaction is unique and has obstacles on its path to the finish line. Each buyer and seller situation is different because no property or location is the same or comparable to an earlier property transfer. Only a local real-estate specialist can put all this information into the right perspective and recommend the best and the most profitable path for you.

But even the best real-estate professional will not be able to answer all your questions and give you all possible explanations, because he or she is not allowed to give legal, financial, or tax advice. For these business fields, you have to consult with an attorney, a tax accountant, and a loan officer or professional.

Each of these professionals is a specialist in his or her field, and none can take over the specialized tasks of another. However, in cooperation, these professionals are unbeatable and focused on your goal, a property sale in a foreign country.

We hope that we have answered your questions about the sale of your home. However, if you still have any concerns or open questions, please let us know. We are here for you.

On the following websites, you will find many valuable facts and details about the United States and its people, businesses, and real estate:

- Florida information: www.florida-informations.com
  e-mail: info@florida-informations.com

- Dream properties: www.florida-dream-homes.net
  e-mail: andrea@florida-informations.com

- Author website: www.andreahoffdomin.com
  e-mail: andrea@florida-informations.com

This book is an addition to our existing books on the topics of business, real estate, and culture diversity and differences:

- *Ihre Residenz im Paradies*

- *Your Residence in Paradise*

- *Immobilienverkauf im Ausland*

- *Secrets of the Caribbean Islands—Cayman Islands*

- *Secrets of the Caribbean Islands—Jamaica*

- Our picture books about Grand Cayman and Jamaica

- And even more books currently in preparation!

We are also available as international real-estate specialists for the regions of the United States, Caribbean islands, and Europe, and available as keynote speakers for events and presentations.

Sunny greetings from the Sunshine State, Florida!